What Lies
Beneath
the
Sunflowers

SHELLEY WYCKOFF

authorHOUSE®

AuthorHouse™
1663 Liberty Drive
Bloomington, IN 47403
www.authorhouse.com
Phone: 1 (800) 839-8640

Published by AuthorHouse 07/25/2018

ISBN: 978-1-5462-5095-1 (sc)
ISBN: 978-1-5462-5094-4 (e)

Dedication

To my God sent mate James Edward Wyckoff for being my partner in life and love and trials.

To my father James Rice an example of hard work and perseverance.

To my mother Anna Lee Tate-Rice a true model of kindness.

To my daughters Elita and Shamolie, who always encouraged my poetry.

To my granddaughters Sydney Kai Jones and Sage Madison Jones for their genuine love.

To my brothers and sisters who continue to encourage me to grow and express my heart and soul.

Contents

Identity

You made your beds, breakfast done
I rolled up my sleeping bag and ate my last orange
You walk the girls to the bus
I walk them to the coop
Your lunches made and in hand
Lunch is a luxury I no longer have

Off to work to get there by 7 am
I have to be out of the shelter by 7:30
Traffic is heavy but not too heavy
For me, I start my walk on these streets
Only 15 minutes late, wonder if my boss noticed.
Will that affect me up for that promotion?
I have no watch or phone to keep track of time.

Rush to be there to pick up the girls from the bus stop
When will I get my child back in school?
Hmmm, her uniform is short and getting too small,
I'll order a new one along with new pants
We wear both of our only shirts and pants we
Own, this much we know
Homework time approaches, but not before dinner.
Tacos
Or chicken parmesan might be a winner
Can we make it across town before cut off dinner is served
Who are you?
Who Am I?

Oh yeah, that's right, I was you 6 months ago

Soldiers

Brave men and women
Young and old from across the globe
Some losing their lives and others bearing lasting debilitating injuries
For causes unknown
Hiding in ditches and trenches for protection
against powerful explosives
Peeping at pictures of love ones that may never be seen again
Full of tremors while trying to be brave
Some returning with one leg..no legs…one arm..no arms
Minds once active and sharp… now dull
or gone by the shattered metal
Eyes once bright now dark like midnight
Sleepless nights as dreams of bombs and terror
and brave men and women killed, slaughtered and
tortured play vividly like a continuous movie
Making their bodies shake with uncontrollable tremors
Brave soldiers who will never be whole again but still
happy that they served our beautiful country.

Skin and Bones

I had thick dark hair but styled to contend with the superficial trends
Smooth and clear skin, but thin and defenseless to words of criticism
I carried a chip on my shoulder
Now nothing but gravity weighs them as I have
shed grudges and past hurts and insults
Tight neck stretched with worry for the unknowable future
Deep dark eyes that searched for faith
Strong arms and legs that carried me from one trial to another
Clean fingernails from not yet digging deep within myself for truth
Meat and muscle on my arms and legs but nutritionally lacking
Quick stepping feet and legs in order to keep up with the Joneses
Now my hair is matted and thin and styled
to flatter my personality and
character
Skin so thick, dagger like words never penetrate
Lifetime of confidence has left lines and lines on the skin
Eyes with a new depth that reaches back in time and sees by faith
Nails dirty with soil from digging to get at our roots
Roots of identity, roots of my family, roots of my problems
Toes with fungus from having walked in countless person's shoes
Stick like legs move slow, steady and deliberate as my path is clearly set
by God (to ensure each step has been preset by God)
Once upon a time I was whole and healthy
Now…I am broken, divinely reshaped and
infused with purpose and peace
Now I am skin and bones,…bones and skin
I am bones – a foundation, support and strength to those in need
I am skin – a covering of love to anyone that encounters me
Yes, now I am finally … and gratefully… skin and bones…

Naked

Like the bare trees in the winter cold
Liquid dripping from my nose like icicles

I look around for a little flame
Brown withered grass plastered to the ground
shielding and protecting
the bugs and other crawling creatures
Like me, the squirrels scramble for food

Cold rain fall on my body parts and chill me within
I am Naked

Though I wear tattered, dirty clothes, no socks
and molded shoes
Chest and booty peering through my clothes
I am naked…inside and out
I am Naked… but I am Human

Dear Santa

I know you're making many stops through the sky, over
mountains and miles of dirt and concrete roads
Bring cheer to the young and old
Black and white
Women, men and children
Baptists, Methodists, Presbyterians, Catholics, sick and
shut in and others
Big gifts, medium gifts and small gifts
Wrapped and unwrapped
Heavy and light
expensive and not expensive
to the rich and the poor
Now....
I need you to stop by my place
In alley #4 where there are no houses, no names on mailboxes,
No lights, no warm heat in the winter cold, no cool air
in the summer heat, no stoves and refrigerators
No soft beds and clean covers
I really need
a heavy coat and cap, shirts, pants, gloves
long johns, underclothes, socks, shoes
soap, wash rag, lotion, bug killer and
anything else that you think I need.
I'm down and out. I'm homeless and alone.

Thank you,
Mr. Homeless

The Resting Place

Countless books line rows of shelves
Books about health, life, love, heroes and villains
Some teach of planting and building and raising children
Providing lectures, instructions, fantasies
Encouraging travel down a path
To change who you are, what you do, and how you think
Tables, chairs and cubby holes to emancipate a mind
Reminders of history and stories of the past…
The library
A place welcoming escape to boundless destinations
For me, it is simply a resting place
Strong, secure and peaceful
Alas, to this I'm not invited
Cause I'm homeless…dirty, tired, hungry and sleepy

My Mother's Womb

I came from my mama's belly
Sleeping, resting, eating and growing for
nine wonderful months
Breathing and kicking and looking and
expecting to be loved and protected….
With high hopes and thoughtful dreams that never came true
Now, I want to return to her womb…the soft,
warm, safe, protective womb.

I Lost it All

I had a good job from 9 to 5
6 days a week
Not knowing how quickly things can turn bleak
I put food on my table, kept the lights, air and heat on,
Never skipping a beat
I needed a little pick me up just to get me through a shift

Didn't sleep well last night
That's all, no big deal for a one time fix
But that fix turned out to be a friend
who came whenever I called
and miraculously made me forget I had any problems at all

Never mind the needles, the sneaking, the deceit,
No friendship is ever really free
The crash and burn of my relationships and job didn't bother me
They just didn't understand
They just couldn't see
But it was me
It was me that couldn't see
My best friend was actually my worst enemy
And now that I've lost it all
I ask myself is there anyone to help when someone falls

In the Dark

I lay down in the depth of darkness
Fighting and shooing hungry rodents that try to feed
themselves on the meaty parts of my body.
Sleeping with one eye open for crawling snakes that
put their poisonous spit in my veins
…In the dark

Digging spiders who try to make a home in the depths of my
ears
In the Dark…

Skunks spraying their funk juice when they think I'm the
enemy
In the Dark…

I'm homeless and fight and fight and fight
Sometimes losing the battle
In the Dark

Wish List

I wish I had…
a car to see the city,
to go to the grocery store, and run errands
A house with a porch to gaze at the rising sun and the moonlight
and stars sprinkled throughout the dark sky

I wish I had…
clear sight to see the flowers of many colors,
the birds, butterflies, and squirrels playing in the yard
Flowers saluting the sky

I wish I had…
strong bones and legs
good Friends and loving family
I wish… I wish… I wish…

The Mirror

I look in the mirror and what do I see
Tired, neglected, rejected, abused, misused

I look in the mirror and what do I see
One who has weathered the storms, bone chilling
bitter cold and scorching heat

I look in the mirror and what do I see
one who eat left over scraps from garbage cans, restaurants, picnics,
parks and dirty streets
Not caring if your spit is all over the scraps
I look in the mirror and what do I see
Scaly feet covered with bunions and cuts as I walk
from place to place searching for shelter to rest my
weary bones

I look in the mirror and what do I see
One who is hated by man but loved by God

I look in the mirror and what do I see
Me…the homeless

Sunday Morning Blues

Stale bread and cold thick black coffee
Fill my stomach but does not satisfy
This feeling must last till dinner time
Stomach churning loud
Headache raging in my head
But it's Sunday morning

Arms weak and legs cramped
My mind says go, but my legs say no
I look around for clean clothes and shoes and none
are found.
But...but...
But it's Sunday morning and I can't go to church.

I Dream

I close my eyes under the bridge, in the woods,
behind restaurants, in the park, in old cars and
Then I dream

I dream of a bed with clean sheets and blankets
Wrapped around a mattress filled with soft
feathers in a house made of wood and stone
I dream of delicious aromas of food cooking in the kitchen
Then....
I wake up trembling and scared when I find
that I'm still unprotected from the roaring, fierce
winds, cold biting snow and burning sun and
I still have a growling, empty, painful belly
I am still alive, but homeless and hungry

The Shelter

Happy faces welcome us
Building is crowded with us...
Happy to be inside...
Sheltered from the cold snowy night
Hot soup, crusty bread and deep black, strong coffee all
Ready for us to partake

I am so happy...we are all so happy
Then we heard their voices...heard their rules
"No drinking alcohol, no drugs, no smoking, no sex, no TV, no radio
no wetting the bed
No roaming through the night"
We have rules...

"Our doors close at 9 pm and you gotta leave by 7 am..."
Rules, rules...more rules

I gotta go...I gotta go
I gotta leave this warm, safe shelter that has
too many rules

Tuesday

Quick!
Someone tell me what day it is.
Is it the day generosity pulls in under the overpass?
Trucks of love roll into position
Delving out spoonfulls
of kindness and
Full plates of hope to fill my hungry belly
Hungry not only for protein but
spiritual nutrition that last much longer
and fills my every fiber
Through bins of clothing items,
they also hand out dignity
some dignity disguised as shoes,
dignity as clean underwear and clean socks for my children
As the loudspeaker comes on and prayer commences,
I am being wholly fed
And now I am peaceful and filled with gratitude…
for the people who serve us on Tuesday under the bridge.

The Blues

I sing the blues when I feel down and out
When I look at my life and see wasted time and energy
When I see my life as one storm after another
Many lovers that come and go that make me feel down, down, down
To the bones
Because I am so lonely and empty
Tears flow in the house and outside when I get sad
Because my love has walked away and
when my man treats me like wasted sugar on the floor
The blues are all about lost love, mistreatment but hanging in there,
Loving another when he supposed to be loving me and
Two timing with me and another
The blues are all about no money and being broke
No respect, no commitment
When I get the blues I take colorful pills
Snort the white stuff and stick the needles into my veins
I have been told that I have a beautiful soulful voice
And have been awarded many medals
Inducted in the Hall of Fame
And given many kudos and media coverage
I'm still sad and have the blues.

(Call me the Blues Woman)

In My House

In my house I see big cracks in the walls
Where roaches make their home
Big holes where mama rats give birth to lots of babies
Their feet making prints in the grease left in my skillet
on the stove

In my house the carpet is matted with dirt, oil and outdoor dampness
Dirty dishes piled high and
wet clothes hanging on the wobbly furniture
but…
In my house I dream, yes I dream of crisp white cabinets,
clean ceramic tile floors, beautiful strong oak furniture,
beautiful bunches of colorful flowers,
happy faces and lively music

My Black People

Picking cotton in the summer heat
Old junk cars all over the yard
Drinking liquor and lying at funerals
Feeding and sitting with the sick
Free room and board for kin folk travelling
From Mississippi to Chi-town
Grannies raising children
Making ice cream in a hand turned freezer
Cooking neckbones, chicken backs, chitlins, fish heads,
Collard greens and fried corn
My Black People

Damaged

We drank the vital, clear liquid
from our faucet each day…
Thinking that it was hydrating our veins and organs
and helping the tiny seed in my tummy grow strong
Thinking that we were washing germs away
and clearing our dark pee and
thinking that the clear water was softening our skin
Because of the lead laced water,
my children will not reach their full potential
for their brains are damaged by the poisonous lead…
They will never think and do
because they drank the toxic lead based water
Damaged…Damaged…Damaged for life

Weeping

My heart is full and heavy
As I weep for the children of many nations
Who know nothing but fighting
Know nothing but hunger
Know nothing but squalor
Know nothing but fear
My tears flow like an open fountain
As I weep for the children of many nations

Lady Bugs

You are like the measly, shameless, relentless, little lady bugs
Squeezing and slipping through my cracks, windows and doors
To mingle with my love, to crawl all over my love
Licking and intertwined…
You come when I'm not home…
Through the night and all day long

Thankful

I'm thankful for God the creator,
Sunrise and sunset – the moon and stars
Wind that blows,
Snow, rain, sunshine
Ocean, rivers, lakes, mountains
Patience and humbleness
Clothes, food, shelter
Family, friends, companions
Knowledge, truth, wisdom

Thankful… Thankful… Thankful

Bed Bugs

I happily entered a five star hotel smiling happily as I
Anticipated a restful time at this expensive high rated hotel
Still smiling I looked forward to an immaculate room
Bedspreads, sheets and pillowcases seamed fresh
Spotless and wrinkle free
Furniture was polished and shining with no signs of dirt or dust
Soft sofas and chairs seemed freshly cleaned and odorless
Closets roomy and filled with neatly folded extra clean linen
I quickly laid my suitcase on the floor, my shoes beside the
Bed and my purse on the beautiful upholstered furniture
Happily I crawled into the bed for a long nap
Only to open my eyes later and saw little brown bugs lined
up on the edge of the mattress and on the sheets
Red spots of blood on the pillows where I mashed
them under my head while I slept and dreamed
The room looked clean but was not clean
Cause the little nasty brown bed bugs were
waiting to crawl all over me
I quickly packed my bag, left the room and demanded a refund

No Good

You are my man
No good, but I love you anyway
I love your smile, your hugs, your sweet kisses and all of you
But….
You treat me so bad
You spend my money,
You don't pay the rent and don't buy any food
You cheat on me
You beat me
You are no good and I know you are no good
But….
I love you anyway

Dead Caregivers

Doctor appointments that must be met
Picking up medicine from the pharmacy
Giving medicine morning, noon, and night
Changing diapers wet from urine and loose stools
Bathing frail, wrinkled bodies covered with sores
Massaging aching joints
Encouraging words for the down in spirit,
Patience for the grouchy, mean and ungrateful
Lifting heavy bodies day and night…
Turning them left and right to prevent sores
Constantly taking blood pressure and temperature
Day in and day out… year after year we see
Dead Caregivers

Awesome

Morning light that gently and quietly follows the dark night
Puffy clouds like cotton in the sky
Stars sprinkled throughout the deep dark sky
Flowers with their beautiful faces salute the hot sun
Trees dressed in their green coats in the spring and summer
after being naked during the winter's cold
The wind whispers in my ears
The rain falls and cleans the air
Birds singing and playing during the day and sleep during the night
Majestic mountains stand tall overlooking the valleys
Deep wide forests stand thick and high
Awesome…awesome God the creator made it all

Broken But Beautiful

Some broken in spirit
Others broken in body by heart disease, cancer,
strokes, liver, kidney, drugs, and
Other diseases
Reactions to medications meant to heal affect the body and mood
Crying day and night for what use to be but no more
Memory loss and confusion
A life sitting and watching but not moving
Fear implanted like a fertile growing seed within
Fear of walking down the street
Of riding in cars and flying in airplanes through the clouds
Fear of dancing the cha cha, the swing, the Salsa
Fear of closing my eyes and never seeing the sun rise again
Sweet companionship now diminished
A common load no more
Once peace and joy now constant irritation
Although not the 100 per cent we once were
but trying hard to be the best that we
are now
Broken, but still alive, whole, still functioning and beautiful

Speckled Cornbread

I get real excited as the aroma of hot cornbread fills the kitchen
With great anticipation
I wait for the sweet taste of butter, milk and
cornmeal blended together
As I take a bite of this feel good bread
I found delicious little crunchy crackling bits throughout my bread
Soooooo..good

Rodeo

Tempers flare
Tears flowed and flowed and flowed
Fists folded tight into round balls
Words said that burned and touched my soul
Then silence and uncomfortableness
Name calling and finger pointing
Sleepless nights
Lack of commitment
No sense of responsibility
Deep depression
Very little or no lovemaking
With all of this, I'm struggling within
As I accept the fact that our marriage is a rodeo
Will we stay in the saddle or fall to the ground?
Our marriage is a rough, tough rodeo

Performance Matters

History is taken and shared later for the world to see
We must perform at our best at all times
Especially since our performance can and
will affect what we cherish most
Performance matters a lot
Watch me.
Watch me closely

I Did Not Know Him

I saw a handsome ebony face
with skin as soft as velvet
His dark eyes laced with long curled eyelashes
Quiet easy movements and a quick tongue
telling me what I wanted to hear
But… I did not know him

Beautiful words flowed from those sweet lips
Excellent command of the English language he had
Great insight into complex situations
But …I did not know him

Carefully hiding his true self
Masquerading as an ideal human being
He came into my life for a brief time
And created grief and havoc
I did not know him
I did not know him at all

Sisters Are Forever

Together, we were silly, we were serious
We danced, we sang,
We fought, we made up

Together, we mourned, we celebrated
We cooked, we ate,
We worked, we played

Together, we traded recipes, we baked
We failed, we succeeded
We shared dreams, we shared realities

Together, we had hope, we prayed
We decried, we praised
We took, we gave

Together, we grew up, we had families
We laughed, we cried
We hated, we loved

We shared all of these things
Together…..because
Sisters Are Forever

A Shiny Ornament

I cried big tears
For a beautiful bright eyed girl (me)
Who thought she found love at last

He was like an exquisite shiny ornament
On the outside
But a thin shell of a person inside
With illusions of grandeur
Radiating at first sight

Proud to be with him,
I followed him from here to there and everywhere,
But found out later he was fragile,
insecure and unstable

He was a shiny fragile ornament

Night Ride

Tonight my body aches and my mind is at its lowest but…
I feel soothed and calm as I ride through
the country roads and highways
Where all humans and animals seemed to be
quiet, hiding, or sleeping
fighting or loving
I take a night ride because
I can't sleep…My eyes are wide open

What Can I be ?

Teacher, teacher
I want to be a teacher
No, no black girl you can't even read

Teacher, teacher
I want to be an artist
No, no black girl you can't even draw

Teacher, teacher
I want to be a ballerina
No, no black girl you can't even twirl

Teacher, teacher
I want to be an actress
No, no black girl you can't even talk

Teacher, teacher
I want to be a writer
No, no black girl you can't even spell

Teacher, teacher
What can I be?
You can come to my house
and do all my cleaning,
wash my clothes and cook my food
That's what you can be

The Gambler

I left home with a pocket full of money
Went to the dark, smoke filled, funky room
Laughed and joked with Mac and Joe
Seeking to win big for my sweet lady
Hours I stayed in the dark dingy,musty room
But my luck was bad and I came home
Smelling of reefer and old cheap liquor
With no rent money and no money for food
To the knife of my sweet lady love.

The Bed

In my old, creaky and stinky bed
My feet are touching other feet
My legs are folded under
Cause there's little room in my bed
for so many legs
Snoring and hot spicy breath blowing in my face
Wet from sister's pee during the night
I'm sad and mad
Help me mama…please
I need my own bed
PLEASE….MY OWN BED

Thanks

I sat in the church house
clapping my hands
singing good songs
stomping my feet
dropping my wig
ripping my dress and stockings
as I jumped the benches and fling my arms
thanking and praising my God for his grace and mercy

My Tab

Go on down to the grocery store
and get me some fish heads, fat back,
a can of mackerel, a can of biscuits
and a bottle of syrup
Give this note to Mister Mundie
And tell him to put these on my tab
Hurry now
Cause we need to eat
Tell him to put these on my tab
I'll pay him next month

Lazy

In the spring I watch the flowers bud and bloom
During the hot summer I sit under the big Oak tree
and swat the flies away
Winter, I sit in my chair by the window and
watch the cold rain and snow all day long and night
The brown leaves wither and fall like rain
from the trees
I love to see and feel them all day long
I'm not going anywhere cause I'm lazy
I'll keep on sitting and looking
Sitting and looking
Cause I'm lazy…real lazy

Busybody

You're here, there and everywhere
Listening to this, that and the other
Talking about nothing
But fishing for more
Shut your mouth
Leave me alone and go get a job
Get a job…any job

Work

Everyday I walk out the door
and work from 9 to 5
Keeps me from idleness
and lusting after the Queen Bee
Don't get many dollars
but enough to feel like a man and
to feed my lady love

The Hotel Room

Beautiful framed pictures of colored exotic flowers
Unique lamps and heavy furniture
Mirrors of varied shapes and sizes
Chairs wrapped in inviting fabric that conceal germs and
dirt and hide tiny little creatures
Bed covers that look immaculate
but feel like bed bugs are hiding in the creases
Floors carpeted, but dirty
Feel like shoes should be worn at all times
instead of bare feet
A TV with limited stations
Bathroom filled with soap, lotion, shampoo
and tissue paper collected and taken home
Towels that look clean
but have washed and dried the bodies of many people
from many corners of the earth...
The sick, the contagious, and the healthy
I enter the hotel room armed with
sweet smelling fragrances, spray disinfectants, germ killer,
house shoes, my own bed covers and towels
I'm prepared

Humble pie

Mississippi born and raised
Gentle as a spring breeze
Beautiful like touch-me-nots and sunflowers
Generous to all who crossed her path
Fruits of the spirit she was endowed
A top notch chef without a degree
She fried chicken backs, chicken wings and fish heads,
Cooked rice pudding,
collard greens and blackeyed peas
Baked sweet potato pies, pound cakes and tea cakes
She was something – and someone- very special
She was a treasure in everyway
Her name was Anna Lee
But…I call her humble pie…
Unforgettable humble pie
Yes, my unforgettable humble pie
My mama

My #1 Fan

Sitting on the front row at each game
Cheering me on when I'm losing
Jumping high when I score
Mad at the coach when he put me on the bench
Yelling until your voice is sore
Mad at the referees when they made a bad call on me
Wearing my name on your shirt and hat
You are My #1 Fan
My daddy

Family is ...

Hope when you feel hopeless
Calming when the storms of life are raging
Triple A when your car breaks down
Assistance when you feel helpless
Loving when you want affection
Supportive when you lose your job
Stingy when you can't stick to a budget
Freedom when you are incarcerated
A listening ear when you need emotional support
There with you when your child is sick
In grief when death occurs
Comfort when you are lonely
On your side when your partner is unfaithful
A refuge when your house burns down
A cab when you can't drive anymore
A guiding light when you lose your vision
Your prosthetic when your legs are amputated
Your rehab when you have heart surgery
Joy and happiness when you live in a nursing home
Irreplaceable when you learn that you have a terminal illness
A home cooked meal when you are hungry
Prayer Warriors when you need prayer
Confidence when self-esteem is low
Unconditional love and collective problem-solving
There for you throughout crisis after crisis
Family is L-O-V-E!!
And Family is......Never Dull!!

My Caregiver

Reminded me about God's love for me and his
forgiveness over and over and over again
Told me how to be born again
and about healings and miracles
Reminded me about God's abounding grace and sweet mercy
Kept the ice chips coming to cool my feverish body
Lifted me and turned me with the
gentleness of a baby
Spoke kind words with a gentle, soothing voice
as I cried long and hard when in pain
Gentle touch when I cussed her out
Showed great patience as I wet and soiled my bed and clothes
Re-positioned my pillows
many times during the day and night
Scraped the caked, ashy scales from my feet and
rubbed soothing salve on my aching body
As I looked into those deep, caring, wrinkled,
watery, tired eyes I whispered....
Thank you, thank you, thank you
My Caregiver

I Love Me

My skin is black and smooth
Elbows ashy, hair nappy and thick
Teeth yellow and crooked
Feet wide with knots on top
Scars on my forehead, legs and arms
Wide nose, wrinkled hands
But, I love me

Boody round and fat
Hips wide
Tummy big and bloated
Tits looking to the ground
Knees fat
Yes, I love me
I love all of me!

All over him

They wined and dined
At the Dew Drop Inn
And later intertwined at the Lay Motel
They stayed until the roosters crowed
When he returned to me…he had no words
Words were not needed
Because his breath smelled like stale fish
Eyes glossy and heavy from lack of sleep
Red lipstick on his face and ears
Cheap perfume all over him
As he dropped his soiled, unzipped britches
Our eyes met…but words didn't come
Because he smelled of her
She was all over him

I am Who I am

My smile is broad – I laugh out loud
My voice is soft and soothing
My steps are quick as lightning
But my heart is troubled
My mind is flooded with evil deeds and deep hatred
My mind is always in a deep dark place
People see me as honorable and decent
But I am who I am

Love and Dedication

I feel your tender touch
I see love for me in your eyes
Lips that speak of God's goodness and protection
Ears that listen closely to my faded voice
Heart that show patience, kindness and
forgiveness
Feet that race back and forth to fetch
water, juice and morsels of food
Arms that hold me tightly and rock me to sleep
Hands that dry my flowing tears
Strength that you have to turn my bruised body from side to side as
you change my sheets when my pee came
down and loose bowels overflowed
Loving arms that provide warmth during cold days and nights and
hours and hours of pain and healing

Merci Beaucoup… Merci Beaucoup my mate
for your endless
love and dedication

Watch Your Mouth

Filthy hurting words
Lying
Accusations
Cursing
Bragging
Snitching
Gossiping
Blaming
Deadly

Watch it, watch it, watch it
Watch Your Mouth
Cause…
When its out you can't take it back

The Majestic Pine

Pine trees thick and tall
With pine needles and cones dropping like rain
Covering the grass like a thick brown blanket
That protects the bugs and rodents
from the cold and windy elements
Winter would not be winter
Without their majestic beauty
Overseeing the brown grass and
White snow blanket

May Day

Decades later I reflect on good times that
make my heart jump with joy
When children were happy and innocent
Girls dressed in frilly dresses
Boys in new shirts and shoes
Outfits cut from the same pattern
Shiny faces and clean bodies
Too excited to open books
Anticipation of dancing in sync around the maypole
Popcorn, snowballs, and juicy hot dogs
With youthful excitement overflowing
We danced around and around
Wishing this fun could last forever
These days of youthful innocence
Long gone and never to return

Body Changes

My flat chest went from tiny knots to big knots
Hair sprouted like a porcupine under my arm pits and covered my gina
Pimples decorated my face
Dreams of boys kissing my lips
Strange new feelings and urges in my mind and in my gina
Then…
I felt the wetness of my panties and skirt
Looked down and saw a big ruby red circle
My body changed from child to woman

Matters of the Past

The movies in my life are continuous
as they show mistakes and more mistakes
missed opportunities and carelessness
Acting like demons have a hold on me
Detours I've taking only to find pain and suffering
Hurts I've inflicted …
Past loves long gone
Friends few and past memories
Failure and isolation I found
Rough, ignorant and stubborn
Emulating awful and dangerous mannerisms
Buried deep within me are horrors of my past
They are matters of the past…that still lives
fertile and alive in my soul

My Grandma's Bible

Decayed, torn, crumpled, faded and fragile
from days and nights of turning
Pages to search for God's instructions for our lives
The goodness of God, God's grace and mercy
The joy of living as servants of God and disciples of Jesus Christ
Helping others in need is obedience to God
That God is our refuge and fortress and that
we should put all of our trust in him
Her pages were folded with deep creases outlining the
fruits of the spirit...love, joy, peace, kindness, patience,
goodness, faithfulness, gentleness, and self-control
Explanation of the fruits of the spirit ...that they are
attributes of persons living in accord with God and all of
us should strive to show daily in our interactions and
That we strive to have virtues of charity, meekness, faith and chastity
Weathered, tattered and torn
In her hands daily
Holding her Bible close to her heart

Still Alive

Little hair that's white as snow
Eyebrows filled with specks of white
Eyes dim
Wooden cane in one hand
holding up wobbly legs and aching back
pants sagging and zippers wide open
skin with deep creases
weathered by life's trials
loose, dangling skin under the neck
using lots of diapers to catch the pee and poop
little or no appetite
food dripping down the chin
sleepless nights and flowing tears
say what is on the mind
Old, Very Old, But Still Alive

Aging Sulks

Wigs and weaves
Hair in patches
Skin sagging
Legs aching – back pain
Memory fading
Temper flaring
Different colors and shapes of pills
for my head, stomach, legs and memory
Smelly salves to quiet the pain
that lingers night and day
Epson salt to loosen the bones
Legs and hands swelling like big balloons
Vagina dropping – penis soft
Eyes dimmer
Ears clogged
Spaced teeth and no teeth
Steps shorter and slower – thin skin on legs
Scaly feet and curled, rotten and fungus toenails
Flu shots and lots of visits to my doctor
Diet now basically is Ensure, Gatorade and prunes
What am I to do?
Aging Sucks

Menopause Queen

I say what I want … things I couldn't say before
I go places now that I didn't dare to go
I wear what I want…dirty or clean
Pressed or not pressed, long or short
Skin tight or loose
Matching or mismatch, checkered or flowered
I eat what I want…
Pig feet, collard greens, cakes, pies
I drink what I want…milk, juice, beer, wine
White lightening, Boones Farm and vodka
Cause I'm a Menopause Queen

No Mamm

I helped mama put the groceries
on the check out counter
The cashier asked mama if she needed anything else
Mama said "no mamm", "No Mamm"
This is all for now mamm
Mama was seventy-eight years old and
The cashier was seventeen

Waiting

I rush through the fast traffic
To get to the white coats on time
Since I'm hurting from head to toe
I check in at 10:10 for a 10:30 am appointment
And join 8 more hurting folks who are also waiting
for the same appointment
While waiting
We share the history of our illness, family illness
And how bad we feel
We speak of medicines and homemade remedies
It is11:45 and we're still waiting
Mad at the doctor…but too sick to leave
We are all too sick to leave so we
continue to wait and wait and wait
Waiting for the Doctor
But too sick to leave

My Black Feet

Those black feet with scaly knots
Resting on top of fat toes and thin toes
With splitting, broken and stained toenails…
Crooked and straight
Knots make wearing shoes so painful
Heels cracked from years of walking barefoot
And running without shoes on dirt and rocky roads
Skin is white, scaly and hard
Inviting unknown viruses to take control

My Black Feet

Big Black Legs

My black legs have many stories
Big scars from falling on cement
while running from the neighbor's dog
Deep gashes from sticky bushes
and climbing through barbed wire fences
Permanent deep, swollen gashes from
the extension cord used by daddy
to make me a decent human being
If my black legs could talk

Fire Pit Night

Night breeze blowing...cool to my skin
Stars sprinkled throughout the dark sky
Bugs sleeping...mosquitoes hiding
Frogs hiding and napping...squirrels nesting in the trees
The sweet sounds of Luther, B.B., Aretha,
Lionel and Whitney in my ears
as flames dance happily in the pit
My mind is thankful and relaxed
as I think of years past and years to come

Sleepless Night

Tonight I'm restless with thoughts scattered like stars in the sky
And my mind is full of memories that I thought were long gone
I try to change the station in my head but the
same painful pictures are everywhere
I toss and turn in bed like a piece of paper moving by a strong wind
Out of control, I put my clothes on, get in my truck
and drive down the dark country road...going
nowhere in particular, but going somewhere
I feel soothed and calm as I ride
down the long isolated country roads gazing at the big round bright
moon and admiring the bright stars sprinkled throughout the sky
My eyes wide open
while
Others are sleeping

My Pocketbook

Lipstick, bobby pins, safety pins, paperclips
Ink pens, pencils and old receipts
from the grocery store and clothing stores
Eyeglasses, credit cards and picture ID card
Candy, gum, cough drops
Notes, letters and forgotten bills
If you want to know me
My life story is in my pocketbook

Silent Pain

I ain't got no family
I ain't got no home
I ain't got no hugs and kisses
I ain't got no claps and hurrahs
I ain't got no smiles
I ain't got no self-esteem
I pretend a lot
I laugh when I'm crying inside
I'm not good enough
I'm moved from place to place
I'm a foster child who hurt inside
But nobody knows

Flowers

All occasions for Valentine, Christmas, birthdays,
engagement, marriage and more
expressing
Love to mama, daddy, sisters, brothers, and friends
Congratulations for new birth, retirement, graduation
anniversary, new job
Death – loved ones, friends, co-workers, church members
All colors, big and small, round and tall
Roses, tulips, gardenias, lantanas and more
So beautiful…So versatile
So different
So Sweet
So elegant for all occasions

Papa

Papa was a rambling rose
Tall in status and high yellow skin
He plowed the fields and planted seeds
Picked the cotton in the hot sun
Fed the hogs and the chickens
All while he thought of his hot lady love
Grandma hid his pants in the loft
To keep him from going to the bed down the road
But Papa had spare trousers
That he wore most nights as he
Walked quickly down the road to his hot, hot lady love

Beautiful Brown People

My beautiful brown people picked cotton
In the summer heat
Kept old junk cars and trucks in the yard
Full of wild animals, cats and snakes
Making their home in a cool, quiet, protective place

Drinking liquor and talking loud at funerals
Sitting day and night with the sick
Providing room and board for kinfolk
leaving the Mississippi black belt
for a life in East Saint Louis and Chicago
Kinfolk sharing beds, food, clothing
Grandma raising children
Ice cream made in the hand turned freezer
Neckbones, chicken backs, fish heads,
Chitlins, collard greens, corn bread and fried corn

My People
My Beautiful Brown People

Country Living

My folks chopped the hard dirt in the fields from sun up to sun down
picked cotton, cleaned house, ironed clothes
Made bread and gravy out of flour and water
Syrup out of sugar, butter and water
Shelled peas, shucked corn, canned fruits and veggies
Raised hogs and chickens
Baked squirrels and rabbits in delicious brown gravy
Made quilts out of scraps from old clothes
Helped family and neighbors
Prayed for the sick
Country living was both peaceful and trying
Their hands were frail, wrinkled and hard
from Country Living

Thank You Letter

Thank you Mr. Booker T. for….
A well-rounded educational experience
Hiring gifted teachers
Buildings that were home away from home
Lasting bonds and friendships
Teaching ethical behavior and character building
Opportunities to share, encourage, love and be loved
Teaching us to love our beautiful brown skin and thick nappy hair
Thank you for….
Producing great leaders for our country
Musicians, singers, doctors, nurses,
Engineers, veterinarians, social workers,
Architects, educators, scientists, researchers and more
Encouraging different paths in life
Planting a yard of beautifully dressed trees
That changed colors with the season and
Stood tall, naked and majestic
For long walking paths through the valley that
provided time to develop lasting relationships
Thank you for….
Cooks that prepared food that taste like home
My own bed to stretch out in and to have sweet dreams
A chapel to thank God for his amazing grace
Black student actors and actresses performing in the little theater,
Talented musicians, steppers in the band, skilled athletes
teachers, dorm counselors, and others who
taught discipline, appreciation and love for
Black folk
Thank you forever and more Mr. Booker T. Washington
For these and more
Thank you for beautiful Tuskegee Institute …. I'm much obliged

Me Ma

My me ma had big brown beautiful hands and
Brown thick arms
A Big brown round boody
Brown legs and feet
Spoke broken English and said
Yes maam and yes sir to young and old white folks
Washed and cleaned the white folks toilets and kitchens
With salty sweat dripping down her face
Made their beds, washed their clothes
And thanked them for the hand me down clothes and the leftover
Spoiled food that she brought home to us….
Her little brown grandchildren

Makeup

All shades light, medium, dark brown
Eye shadow dark as midnight
Deep red rouge covering my jaws and
Deep red paint covering my lips
All over my face – thick layers to hide the
tracks of my tears

Beauty Shop

Lots of brown bodies with long, medium and short hair
Thick and thin
Sit quietly from wall to wall
Waiting for a comb out and shampoo
With vigorous strokes and soothing hands
Tingling conditioner for the fragile
Dry scalp and weak hair
Requests made for extensions, braids, twists,
Knots and flat twists
Add a little color and trim my ends
Lots of brown bodies pay
Their money and leave
While smiling
Others leave with tears in their eyes and mouths poked out

Sunday Church Parade

Women wearing
Big hats, little hats, straw hats, no hats
High heels, low heels, no heels
Long dresses short dresses
Fancy shiny dresses and plain dresses
Dressed up, dressed down
Smelling of flower scented bath water and sweet soap
Men dressed in long jacket suits, short suits coats and
Plain shirts with blue jeans
Smelling like British Sterling, Canoe and Old Spice
As they parade down the aisle to listen
To the preacher man

Memories

Memories are flashes from the past
Good, bad, devastating
That never goes away
They come back to haunt us
For a long, long time

Summer Time

Trees bare from winter's cold put on their
beautiful green dresses
Grass once brown, now green
Colorful flowers scattered and crowned
with butterflies kissing their petals
Crickets talk loudly to each other throughout the night
Lightning bugs proudly parade their lights
Birds sing beautiful tunes, fight and makeup
Squirrels chase each other and
Hide their food to eat during winter's cold
Fields and fields of sweet corn filled with milk
Strong green okra, beans, and peas
Ripe red tomatoes, plums and peaches
long hot green peppers and cucumbers
Big watermelons and cantaloupes
Barbeque grills send out
Delicious smells from
Smoked chicken and ribs fill my nostrils
Hand turned Ice cream freezers filled with ice
Rag smoke fires and mosquito spray used to keep the mosquitoes away
Children playing outside in the moon light and old folks and young
folks sit on the porch watching the moon and making plans
Summer time, my love
How I love summer time

He IS

He shows us how special we are
Holds us close in the warmth of his healing love
Reminds us that he is our bridge over troubled waters
Knows the needs and desires of our hearts
Strengthens us when we are weak
Uplifting when sad
He showers us with blessings, grace and mercy
Dependable when others are some timey
Endless goodness, love and power
Healing touch that comforts and strengthen us
Gives peace, joy and love
Is merciful and steadfast
Is a powerful healer
Forgives our sins over and over
Is compassionate
Is a way maker
Who is he?
He is God

Black Dress

Day or night I'm fine
I fit right in
Dress me up or dress me down
Adorned with pearls or gold
Shoes of the rainbow go well with me
You wear me to church, work or party
Fitted or loose
mini or maxi length
Polyester, linen, silk, cotton
You can't do without me
I'm your little black dress

China

Beautiful as a sunflower
Exquisite as a rose
Artistic glamor like no other
Pleasing to the eye
Delicate and fragile
Dropped, it shatters into a hundred tiny pieces
Never to be put together again
My aching heart is like this china
Fragile, shattered, broken and can't be fixed

Kitchen drawers

In my kitchen drawers
I have spoons, forks, knives, spatulas,
Egg separator, shredders, big soup spoons,
Apple slicers, melon cutters, measuring cups,
Measuring spoons, wine openers, melon baller,
Ice cream scoops, tiny sifters, ladles and more
They are used to create mouthwatering meals
Morning, noon, night and in between
So convenient, so useful, so organized

My Kitchen Drawers

The Cruise

Overjoyed with great anticipation of exploring new countries, new
cities, new waters, different and unique people and customs
With high expectations I stepped on board the
luxurious ship with eyes wide open
The ship so large it seemed to cover an entire block with
tiny boats pinned to the side of the ship assured me of our
safety if we had to quickly evacuate the gigantic ship
Rows of seats on deck for nude bodies to lay in the hot sun
To show their shapely curves or fat
The beautiful sleeping quarters with spacious rooms, beautiful
furniture, immaculate bathrooms and floors were so
inviting for relaxing my weary, tired body and troubled mind
Bountiful assorted foods available day and night that
guaranteed extra pounds on the waistline and hips
Laughing and joking with great anticipation, I settled down
and looked forward to this exhilarating new experience

Wishes for the New Year

I don't want no new car
No mink coat
No new sofa, chairs or bed
No diamonds and pearls
No expensive perfume
All I want for the New year is you
My handsome strong brown man
My brown energized bumble bee with your loving, admiring eyes
Always fixed on me
Always doing for me
All I want for the New Year is you and your love

Tattooed

Neck adorned with flowers and secret words
Arms covered with past and present loves, animals, zodiac signs
Quotes and scriptures
Stomach with favorite cars and past love
Hips and legs with good memories and
Feet with places visited
Tattoos are hiding me from the world
Hiding the real me from the world
I'm tattooed

Body and Mind

Hair matted from sleeping on all sides
And sometimes wild and bushy with debris from
the open window on the bus
Wrinkled and smelly clothes I wear
Eyes glossy from feel good drugs
Prescribed and not prescribed
Eyelids half glued with sticky butter
Eating a bag of chips and brown bananas
A loud constant cough and a runny nose
No books, pen, or paper I bring
I feel empty and have a troubled mind but....
I'm here in class teacher
My body is here...but not my mind

Mama

Loving and generous
Encouragement and praise
Kind to those who crossed her path
Sharing God's promise of spiritual abundance
Believe that we are saved by Grace
A tenderhearted and forgiving heart
Completely humble, patient and gentle spirit
A servant's heart
Yes, you, Anna Lee, my mama

My Love

I can't thank God enough for bringing you into my life
at beautiful Tuskegee Institute in the Fall 1968
Your calmness, insight into situations and
discerning ability has been a real blessing
Your energy, strength, compassion for others
and thirst for knowledge is mind blowing
My prayer today
my Pershing Rifle, my Omega man
is to share many more years with you, my love
My one and only love

Wet Pillow

Dark mascara cover her lids
As water flow like a running faucet from her eyes
When she viewed her child's still, cold, scarred body
From the Mississippi Delta lying stiff and still

Deep scars covered his face, neck, and hands
A permanent dark band around his neck
Made from the noose pulled so tight around his neck

The brown lady that birthed him
Seated like a lifeless iron statue
As friends, family and strangers circled
The box holding her beautiful brown boy

As I reflect and dream and dream
As I think and think some more
My tears flow continuously and
my pillow is wet, very wet for the little brown boy
and his sad, sad mother

Black Sheep

My family is big and filled with
doctors, nurses, teachers and lawyers who
studied long and hard in big fancy schools
throughout the land
But I took the road of troubled company
Thieves, whorehouses and drugs
Living in rat infested houses and dodging flying bullets
In and out of prison and therapy
I am known as the
Black Sheep in my family

Boiling Teapot

Beautiful persons with lots of
Chilling memories of life's tragedies
Locked tight in a glass jar
Raging terror with red eyes and loose tongue
Broke out like a hot boiling teapot with a broken lid

Job Adultery

Long hours I spend with you
Completely engrossed, wanting more time with you
Always thinking about you and your quiet tenderness
I am consumed by your beauty and
I love spending time with you in our special place

Thoughts and feelings complete and fulfilled
Feelings of deep love and appreciation for our
Intertwine, laughter and friendship bonds
Dreams of compliments and kudos
Many excuses for being alone with you
My mind completely relaxed
As I score points with you again and again

Compliments galore I receive
Full intimacy and privacy scheduled
As my mind is filled with thoughts of you...always of you

When I'm with others I'm thinking of you
My eyes and mind never grow tired of you...
My job, my job, I love you

The Parade

Skimpy clothes worn in the crisp cold weather
Dancing bodies and loud music
Queens in tiaras
Kings in shiny tux
Antique cars and new cars
Trotting beautiful stallions
Candied apples
Hot coffee and assorted candy
Tee shirts and caps for sale
I love the Parade

Tears of a Clown

Yes, I pretend to be carefree and funny and happy
Doing funny tricks to please the crowd
I make others laugh when I'm crying inside
Instead of speaking, I use actions and movements

I have my own special face and
Hide behind the makeup packed on my face
Bright colored paints around my sad eyes,
Crooked mouth, thick red eyebrows,
Large red nose and a bushy head of yellow hair
I wear tattered, patched clothes and gigantic shoes
Tears of a clown are private
Because I can't let you see my true self –
The inner me – the real me

You never see my tears cause I cry inside
While wearing a wide grin on my face
These are the tears of a clown

Empty Bed

Sheets still pressed – no wrinkles
I wait one hour, two hours, three hours and longer
No creaking box springs
No touch of legs or hands
No yawning…no sighs...no sounds
No coughing, no chanting…only silence….
Quiet, complete silence
Because you are not here
The bed is still empty

Winter Time

Tire tracks deep into the white stuff
That covers everything that stand still
The house, bushes, cars, lamp poles, mailbox
Dogs and cats slide though the slippery ice
As if they have on skates in a skating rink
Silence is beautiful and nothing moving
Calmness and cozy
It's winter time

Falling Tears

The tears of a weary one fall like rain
Never ending but flowing like a bursted pipe
In sub-zero temperature
Tears flow from depression and physical pain
Humor and laughter which protects the heart is missing
Invisible barriers prevent healing
So the tears continue to fall
Day and night until I'm weary
There are too many tears falling and falling
I'm too tired to stop them so I let them fall

Slavery...Alive?

While soaking up knowledge like a dry sponge
In a puddle of water
Violent, angry voices and rushing uniformed
Men rushed in and interrupted our studies
As if they were about to put out an out of control fire
Mouths were stretched open in awe
As we were snatched up from our seats,
Pushed out of the door and into dirty trucks and caravans
Herded like cattle into captivity
Not knowing our fate...
Would we have to sell our brown bodies
Marry old white men or
Work for pennies as servants
Tears and cries of pain went unheard
No one tried to help
As our mothers gashed their teeth and cried
Never ending tears flowed
like an endless river
The global voices of men, women, and children
Of all statues cried loudly in disbelief and opposition
Kinfolk and strangers cried loudly throughout the country
And abroad that slavery is still alive and well
That the shackles of years ago are as tight as ever
As we bow to the will of our masters

We Matter

Beautiful black men and women
All sizes and occupations
Fathers, sons, brothers
Mothers, daughters, sisters
Married, single, divorced, widowed
Fighting for human rights
Fighting for civil rights
Fighting for justice and valuation of black folks

Anger, passion and hope
That black lives matter
That black lives are important
Beautiful black women, men, and children

We all matter

Hot Skillet

Trees wrapped in fungus
Leaves dark and withered
Lay dying on the ground
Dark clouds up above
Confused mind and broken limbs
Beautiful moments a distant memory
Evident by my shaggy clothes and wild hair
Twisted lips and red eyes
Tossed in scorching heat
Not aware of day or night
No strength or will to pull
Myself out of this hot skillet

Cleaning Day

Mama took three buses from our house
To the white lady's house to clean from top to bottom
She cleaned three bathrooms, four bedrooms,
washed dishes and smelly clothes
Mopped and waxed floors and wiped all windows
The white lady reminded her to clean the refrigerator
And take the bologna, biscuits, sweet cakes, old fruit
To our house
Mama came home tired, very tired with a big bag of goodies,
Old, spoiled, but good.

Sweet and Good Times

Mama's sweet potato pies, jelly cakes and
Rice pudding made my nostrils dance
Her chicken smothered in dark brown gravy cooking
Next to a pot of rice
Collard greens dancing around and around
glued to the meaty neck bones
While white pork was frying in the skillet
Dancing in the hot...hot grease
And chicken backs browned to perfection
These were sweet and good times

Light Skin

Black house servants and black field workers
Fighting each other left and right
Wanting to be lighter than a paper bag
Buying loads of skin whiteners and lotions
For brightening
Feeling energized and superior if light skin
Beautiful, smart, but black get back
No blacks on TV, radio, magazines
Black and ugly – no pride
Devaluing self all the time
Marry light and bright and have light babies
Stay out of the sun if you want to be light
And counted as human beings

If I Could

If I could, I would
Wash the thick layers of powder, rouge and
Mascara from my face

Take the different colors out of my fake hair
Lower my voice when speaking instead
of yelling and cursing
Erase the tattoos from my body
Wear clothes that's not skin tight like
They are painted on

If I could, I would do these things
So that you could see the real me
unveiled

Country Living

With its dark planks with gaps between the planks
Where we could see the dark ground
See rats run and play in and out of the house and bite us in the dark

The pot belly stove filled with wood
Cooked the bread, fried corn and chicken
Mama's sweat rolled down her face
Cause the house was over heated
No freezer to be found
Only a dipper and bucket of cool water

Yards made of hard dirt
Swept daily with the broom
No grass to be found
Where chickens strutted proudly
Dogs slept in the sun and hogs ate the slop

Outhouses dark, tiny and stinky
With hundreds of tiny maggots floating around in the liquid
Mind blowing smells filled the little outhouse
No lingering and reading in there
Hard, hard, hard country living

Faces

Deep creases pressed deeply in my face
From hunger, evictions, loving wrong,
Fighting, rough nightlife
Too many poison needles, swallowing the white powder,
drinking poisonous liquor and living a fast life
Faces show our history
Faces Never Lie

Cold Black Dirt

Beat up, tied up, stepped on, burned, drugged
Abused, misused and lied on
I care not about seeing another beautiful sunrise
or bright moon against the dark sky
Now I welcome the solitude in the big box
covered by the cold black dirt

My Hat

You my love
Shield me from the scorching sun
From the Rain and cold snow flakes
From the piercing, hateful eyes
Lovely to me and useful
My Beautiful Hat

Chemo Day

Quietly and preoccupied in deep thoughts
I sit and reflect today and yesterday about my current state
As the vital liquid enters the canals within
me making me tired and lifeless
I see the green leaves showing their heads on this beautiful
Spring day after sleeping comfortably during the winter
Dormant flowers taking long naps under the
warm dirt covered with the cold snow
Rain showers fall briskly over the dirt and wash the snow away
Homes warmed and cozy by the hot log fires, big
black stoves, gas stoves and kerosene heaters
Lots of cheer, chatter and optimism about plans for warm sunny days
While my eyes are red from flowing tears as my body is full of pain
Nausea and pain take control as I try to forget the vials
of chemo moving slowly throughout my body
But…. An angel despite the raging pain helped me to see the
beauty of God's Universe and amazing Grace and mercy
Therefore I'm thankful for another day

Making a Way

Eight children in a little white house
Slept 3 and 4 in a bed
Wore hand me down clothes from each other and
From cousins and neighbors
Ate meals at different times with mama reminding us
To save some for the last to eat
Daddy's portion was taken out first and wrapped
Tightly in the stove
Our bare feet running down the street
Never slowed by rocks and trash
Played outside until night came
Then inside the house
We went to a little round tin tub of warm waiting water
One after another we cleaned our bodies in the
Same water in the same little tin tub

The Broken Chain

The chain had eight strong links
Different sizes, different shapes, different spirits,
Different talents, different goals, different potentials,
Different experiences, different ailments

Some links shined while others were dimmed
By challenges and struggles

Some fell prey to liquors and mind changing drugs
Some had diabetes, strokes and heart disease
Others were the punching bag of abusive mates

Despite the differences, there was lots of love
Now the chain has a missing link…
Lost on October 11, 2010
A sweet voice we can only hear in our minds
Now the chain is broken, smaller and does not feel right

Macho Man

Standing, twisting, bending, reaching is a challenge
Robustness is long gone
Muscles once big and hard now soft
Infections ravishing within my body
Walking slowly when I use to skip and run
Watching my step cause I don't want to fall
Energy real low
M mind says go and do but my body says no
Weight dropping when I'm eating a lot
Can't do what I use to do
Can't carry grocery bags, suit cases, bricks
Can't paint the house, cut the grass, or spread the mulch
Despite my physical decline ...I don't want to sit and
cry so I'll pump the iron and workout daily
because I'm too macho to be frail

Yes I am

I am a woman
Hardworking
Kind
Gentle
Strong
Talented
Generous
Faithful
Forgiving
Yes, I am
I am, I am, I am
Yes, I am all these and more

Good Eating

Fried chicken backs and fish heads
Tender rabbits laying in a pool of gravy
Biscuits, fat back and syrup
Cornbread crumbled in buttermilk
Mackerel and white rice
Blackeyed peas and collard greens
Rice pudding made from rice leftover from breakfast
Good eating, yes this was real good eating

You, My Addiction

I love you to the moon and back
I love you when the sun comes up and goes down
I love you more than all the stars in the sky
I love you more than hogs love slop
I give you my last dime
Lie and cheat for you
Take beatings from you
Steal for you
Give you my body and soul
Cause I am addicted to you
You are my addiction

Gratitude

I am grateful for......
Jesus Christ who died on the cross for me and others
The love of God
God's grace and mercy
A devoted, supportive spouse
Children with good work ethics
Extended family
Blessings to see a new day
Friends
A forgiving heart
A servant's spirit
A humble heart
A desire to learn more
A roof over my head
Transportation
Yes, I'm grateful, grateful, grateful

Joy

I see beauty
Goodness
Calm instead of chaos
Love not hatred
Peace instead of fighting
Togetherness instead of division
I see healing
Challenges
Opportunities to be creative
Times to bridle my tongue
I see grace daily and am thankful
I see unexpected resources and blessings
I see connections, support and positive relationships
I see fulfillment
I see light despite darkness of some days
I see hope overshadow thoughts of despair
I am grateful when the sun rise each day
And
God's amazing grace and presence in my life
Therefore
I see and I know

Constipation

I eat real good everyday in the big house
I dine on pig feet, pig ears, hog mauls, chitlins, fat back,
Mac and cheese, white potatoes and rice with gravy
It feels so good on my lips and in my throat
As it moves down to my stomach only to
Stop in my zig zag pipes
Big pills, little pills, powdered mixes,
Castor oil, prunes and enemas
Can't loosen the good stuff I've gobbled down
I am constipated
I sit for a long, long time waiting in pain for
my delicious feast to show its face
Help me! Help me! Help me please
I am very constipated

Hospital Blues

Many, many sleepless nights
The voices of hospital workers
who with their sweet voices turned on the light
in the room at different times during the night
to achieve their goal
I heard the same song every night
Time for medicine
Need to get some blood
Want to take your vitals
Want some water?
Want a bath?
Can I help you to the toilet?
Let me fix your pillow
Have you had a bowel movement?
Take this miralax
These are sleepless nights in the hospital

Private Pain

I wear the perfect façade but behind closed doors
There is a salty steady waterfall
That leaves deep stains on my face
They are the result of shattered dreams
and broken promises
The result of numbness and denial
The result of distancing myself
From responsibility and commitment

I wear the perfect façade
For the worries of the day are many
My pain leave me frazzeled and torn and
My brokenness leave me without energy
No one to love me and share or see my pain
Just a bunch of useless grand illusions
I remain ragged and poor in spirit
Because my private pain continues

Dementia

He was a skilled designer of furniture
With money galore
He had a comfortable home in the city
He had dependable transportation and lots of friends
He had access to TV, radio and newspapers
From various states and cities that
Increased his knowledge galore
Stricken with strokes and later the cancer
That greedily ate the colon and invaded the liver
The once vibrant uncle went from a tall, lean man
With a healthy mind and a strong body to dementia and
Skin and bones

Thin

My cracked feet and thin legs moved slowly
Searching every crook and corner for a piece
Of bread, crackers, cereal
No luck
All I found was molded, smelly dog food
But, since I am thin, very thin, and very hungry
I ate it all

Trash Cans

Trash cans are filled with the story of our lives
Information about where and how much is spent,
What has been bought, places we go, and
People we are with
Bills due and bills paid, food we eat
Clothes we buy, movies we watch,
Magazines we order
If you want to know about me…look in my trash can
Trash cans tell it all…all of my secrets …all about my life

Black Sheep

My family is big and filled with doctors, nurses,
Teachers, lawyers, scientists, engineers and educators
Who studied long and hard in those big ivy
League schools throughout the land
But... not me
I took the road of troubled company, thieves,
Whorehouses, jail birds and drugs
Living in rat infested houses, dodging flying bullets and
Waiting for the mailman with my welfare check
I am known as the Black Sheep in my family

Down and Out

Body aching
Blood shot eyes
Hair wild over my face
Skin ashy
Shirt with visible dirt
Pants sagging, torn and nasty
No socks
Shoes too big
With hands stretched out and eyes begging for
Some change, a dollar, two dollars
Cause…
I'm a broken man
Down and out….hungry and tired

Coal Mine

Dark solitude keeps me awake and alert
In this deep, dark cave
With the awareness of its frailness and weak structure
Walking lightly as to not disturb its tender frame
I move slowly and deliberate in the coal mine
Cause
I want to see light again
I want to be with my family

Sweetie

My name is Sue…but as I enter
the grocery store, restaurants, clothing and other stores
All I hear is sweetie, hon and darling
I quickly remind them that my name is Sue
My name is Sue
Not sweetie…not hon…not darling
My name is Sue!

Mississippi Cotton Fields

Mississippi cotton fields stretched for miles and miles
With white fluffy balls that say I'm ready for the picking
So I put on my big wide straw hat and coveralls to
hide my skin from the scorching sun then
Wrap my biscuits and fried salt pork for lunch
and down the dirt road I go to
Pull the white balls from the sticky bushes
All day long
From sun up to sun down

Between the Sheets

As we lay exhausted and tranquil after our fiery intertwine
Touching and feeling the warmth of our bodies and
The wet hair on your back, arms, and legs
Your head in the pillow looking up at the sky and
Approaching daylight, but hating to leave

I admire and love your slender, strong black body
Reminding me of a strong, wild stallion
Now resting after a wild run
Sweet talk and promises that you can't keep
Knowing you belong to another and
That you must leave and run to another
But in my heart and mind
I keep a vivid memory of your body
between the sheets after our wild, fierce, sweet
but
forbidden love

Newlyweds

Bright eyes
Loving glances
Sweet words
Gentle touches
Fiery kisses and long love making
Maybe…we will stay together for years to come
And keep our eyes on each other
And not on other passersbys
We are newlyweds

Fiery Stove

Lots of love and kindness like rich kindling on a fire
Add respect, honesty and commitment and touchy feeling
like big dry wood,
That makes the fire hotter
Perhaps, as the years roll by,
Our love will be like a well fed hot fiery stove

The Cold Dirt

Many, many soulful blues singers are
Now laying in the cold, cold dirt
But…their elegant, smooth, sad voices are still alive
As they make me feel hot all over
and make me want to jump up and down
My heart accelerates
My mind ponder vividly of deep love
Good and bad times
Good and bad love
Stolen love
Lost love
My soulful blues singers are still in my mind and soul
Although they lay still in the deep, cold, cold dirt

Motels

Many, many motels have dingy sheets
Bed bug mattresses and sofas
Germy bedspreads and dirty matted carpets
But still…a place to transition from virgin to whore
A place for rekindled love,
Stolen love, wild unconventional love, baby-making love
And a place to relax, renew and recharge

Chi Town

Shotguns, rifles, hand guns, pistols
Pointed at targets and bystanders
Killing, mutilating and paralyzing adults and children
On the streets, pavement, alleys, yards and cars
Then…parents, sisters, brothers, family and friends
Put on their little black dresses and black suits
To say goodbye as their loved one is locked in a big box and
lowered in the
Deep dark hole and covered with the cold black dirt and
then topped with loads of beautiful, colorful flowers

Recollection

During the midnight hours I toss and turn
Wet with sweat and chilled and sweat again as the
Movie of my life play like a silent movie
My heart beats higher and higher and faster and faster
Making my body and mind exhausted
By the horror of what I recall

I'm Nina

Call me wild as the untamed lion, bold, fearless,
anxious, indifferent, hopeless, sad, impulsive,
Risk taker, moody, abusive, angry, tar baby, lonely,
Loveless, controlled, trapped, powerless, fiery, scary
Call me these and more but I know that…..
I'm beautiful Nina …a beautiful soul
Yes …I'm a beautiful, bold and gifted soul

Deep Sleep

Why do you sleep so soundly
When your doggone pretty girl is in pain?
Why do you sleep so soundly when your
Doggone pretty girl is hurting?
I'm wrenching and rolling in pain, but I
Can't feel a hand, an arm or a tear drop
All I hear is your peaceful, deep deep sleep
As I toss and turn in pain

Unforgettable Prince

He was an unforgettable Prince who was
Young, gifted, and black
He unified, people with his music and
He reminded me of an energized battery
He was….
Uncontrollable
Unforgettable
Incredible
Magical
Charismatic
Creative
Visionary
Private
A Perfectionist
All of these and more…all wrapped neatly
Like a ball of beautiful, colorful, purple, yarn

Gifted

His skin reminded me of smooth light brown caramel icing
Mascaraed eyes dark as the night
Arms dangling with 100 percent energy
Legs kicking in all directions and wiggling like an octopus
Fingers manipulating musical instruments
Rosey lips and cheeks, powdered face
Prissy shirts and high heel shoes
The unforgettable, incredible, breathtaking talented'
magical soul took my breath away and made me feel
warm as hot cake inside
Made me think and feel quiet anticipated love
He was a ball of soft bright yarn
that could not be controlled
as he sang with his lips and made his
instruments sing and move with dynamic
flexibility, balance, strength and endurance
He was called many things-dynamic performer, musician,
smart businessman, dangerous, edgy,mysterious, private,
innovative, unique, compassionate, gifted,
flamboyant, sexy, uncontrollable
Call him what you want
But to me…he was my gifted Purple Prince

Not My Life Song

All of my life, I've heard this song…
You are a star
Lead the way
Be the best
Shoot for the moon
Reach for the stars
Awesome
You are an achiever
You are born to succeed
Believe in yourself
Keep a positive attitude
Strive for the highest excellence
Learn all you can
Dream big
Perseverance is the key
Knowledge is power
And
Stay away from the unfocused, the inattentive,
The followers and the long sleepers
This is my song, my life song written by others…not me
Not my life song

Spoiled Food

The white woman's fridge had so much food
Lots of meat, casseroles, soups, veggies,
Biscuits, cornbread, pancakes, grapes, oranges, apples,
Plums, lots of milk, orange juice, apple juice, prune juice
Mama put it all in a bag, got on the bus and brought it home
For all of her little hungry kids to feast on the spoiled, spoiled food

The Rent Money

You slip quietly through the door
Careful not to wake a soul
Your eyes are red as beets from smoky rooms
Your mouth curved downward with sadness
Clothes wrinkled and foul smelling
As you sat and sat and sat and sat
Until all the rent money was placed on the table
Yours pockets empty…you came home
to me

Photo Albums

A source of history – recording time and events
Love and hate
Inspiration and devastation
Hope and disappointment
Sadness and happiness
Healthy and unhealthy Relationships
Historical Photo Albums
Show pictures of my life

A Loose Cannon and Unloved

I am filled with explosives
All through my head, my veins, my joints, my organs
Not ever wanted, but tossed from one place to another
Never feeling that sense of belonging
Beat down, knocked around
Health conditions unattended
Hate filled words and eyes like daggers
Planting baby seeds without a thought
While trying to love and be loved
Special education or no education
Changing schools like clothes
I'm a loose cannon
I'm a loose cannon, unloved and waiting to explode

No Connections

I'm not just naked, hungry and homeless
I'm unloved, unwanted and uncared for
I'm free as a bird and no one cares if I come or go...live or die
In school or out of school
Happy or sad
Scared or safe
Successful or failing
No goals, hopes, or dreams
No connections, no relationships, no trust,
No security, no love, no one to miss me
I have no connections

I Need Family

I need my family
For support, comfort, interaction, love, safety net, hope,
Money, companionship, friendship, protection,
To share problems, to make decisions,
To share good news and bad news
For making decisions, and to belong
I really need my family

A Bold Free Spirit

A voice within whispers all day and night
She is good, kind, beautiful and gives love unconditionally
She is worthy, special and cared for
She is gifted, She is God's child and
Never afraid to speak her mind
A bold free spirit

Strong in faith
A tireless energy to meet the demands of life
A helping force in the lives of those needing help
A bold free spirit

The goodness of God flows through her
and with her, as she helps women become mothers and
shares the joy of mothers who hear the first cry of their babies
A bold free spirit….My Lollie

I'm Healing

I'm healing from being called ugly
from not feeling wanted
from emotional scars
from physical scars
from having to eat with the flies, roaches, and rats
Don't bother me...I'm healing

Deep Roots

Thank you mama for my deep roots
For the rich blood running through my veins
The message you put in my head about how to love
The poor, the rich, the happy, the sad, the weary
To appreciate folks from all walks of life
To respect their status whatever it may be
To keep ears wide open with active listening and to
be open and objective to views of others
Thank you mama for teaching me that hard work
Feels good and honesty can be sad, but liberating
That serving others in need is Godly,
To sit still in the midst of life's storms
To meditate and think about God's goodness
To dream big and take action
Thank you mama for teaching me to believe in my ability and
To be a source of encouragement to others, to celebrate the
achievements of others, to forgive those that hurt me, to love
others and to accept love and to be patient with the persistent
Thank you dear mama for my deep, deep roots

Black Singers

Sing about heartache
Love
Madness
Repentance
Double crossing
Strength and weakness
Loving when it's wrong
Loving the man next door
Loving the woman down the street
Fire and desire
Racism
Politics
Mama and daddy
Dreams
Black singers are experts in singing the blues

Quilts

Quilts tell stories
Each patch is gingerly laid in a pattern
that shows our life's activities from birth to aged
Some patches are beautiful, reflecting cherished memories
and dreams come true
Other patches bring tears upon reflections of
danger, toils and snares
Still others of blood, and sweat
My quilt is so beautiful, yet filled with drama

Rugs

Lots of colors
Lots of textures
Sizes – wide, narrow, short and long
Colors mixed and solid, bright and dull
Only to be stepped on, laid on and
Left with dirt, grime and grease
Rugs tell the stories of moods and philosophies
Rugs give a historical perspective

Sharing

Death came quickly with the deadly drugs
His kidneys went to Millie
John was thankful for his eyes
His liver to Sam and heart to Little John
He didn't mind sharing cause sharing is caring

Keeper of the Spirit

Love yourself...love your skin
Love who you are
Love your dreams – what you want to become
You are the soul within – not your color, not your texture
You are what you are within
Dark girls rise, dark girls shine
Shine from the inside to the outside

The Raging Storm

I cannot begin to understand the wild storm within me
How long can I last?
My body is not my own, can't seem to make sense of anything
My head, though attached cannot be in the present
But is overwhelmed with what ifs
What if I could rewrite my life script
I am a mess but can't seem to help myself…
Feels like I'm in knee deep mud, but can't move
Why should I feel like an empty abandoned shack…
Like an empty shell that no one can see the true elements
Burning like fire and like a time bomb waiting to explode
How long can I last?
How long…how long can I last?
In this raging storm

Trees

Trees wear their green coats in the summer time
And are naked in the winter
Their bodies are naked and vulnerable to
Winter's ice and stormy weather
The raging wind makes them bow down and bend over with humility
The mildew and Ivey add a different texture and color
Knots and holes, chewed diligently by squirrels, and wild animals
Names inscribed on trees tell tales of love
Beautiful trees… so different

Brown Bodies

Lying in the red stuff on the dirty streets and highways of many cities
Babies in mother's arms taking a stroll down the block
Children riding happily in their cars for a family outing
Other children playing outside in their yards and
On the sidewalk
The beautiful brown bodies lie still and dead soaking in the red stuff
Unable to laugh and play no more

Old and Thankful

Wigs and weaves
Hair in patches of grey
Skin sagging
Legs aching and back pain
Temper flaring
Memory fading
Pills for my head, stomach, legs
Smelly salves to quiet the pain that lingers
Day and night
Epson salt to loosen the bones
Family and friends dying
Vagina dropping
Legs and hands swelling
Eyes dimmer
Ears clogged
Missing teeth or no teeth
Steps slower and shorter
Flu shots
Thin skin
Scaly feet and colored rotten toenails
Drinking lots of Ensure and Gatorade
Being old is a chore
Being old is different
But…I'm so thankful

Winter's Snow

The beautiful falling white flakes cover everything
That stand still
The house, mailbox, bushes, trees, cars, lamp poles, trees
Deep tire tracks in the white stuff
Dogs, cats and other animals slide through the
Slippery ice as if they have on skates in a skating rink
Silence is beautiful and calming and
Cozy and clean in winter's snow

Night Solitude

My tears fall in private in the middle of the night...
Long before daylight when there's perfect quietness
My tears fall like a waterfall...
Continuous...and wet my night shirt,
my gown or other garment used at night
I speak to no one about my continuous pain and
The desires of my heart
Alone and discouraged, I remain, as the pain
continues and the tears continue to flow in
the solitude of the long, long night

Manny – No Nanny

My one and only love worked the day and partial night shift
I worked the midnight shift seven days a week
So I hired a young, beautiful, energetic, bright eyed, woman to
Help me with my children

My job required some travel several days per month
And I was thankful for the sweet, beautiful nanny who
Cleaned, cooked and took care of my children…
Took care of my entire household
My children loved her
My husband loved her and loved her totally – all of her
I should have hired a manny instead of a nanny

Only You

Only you can…
Lift my spirit
Heal my broken heart
Stabilize my shattered mind
Look beyond my faults and see my needs

Only you….
Give everlasting mercies
Forgive me when I sin
my one and only friend when I'm lonely
Rock me to sleep
Carry me when I'm weak
Lead me and guide me everyday

Only you…only you God
Thank you

Papa

Papa was a rambling rose
Tall in statue with high yellow skin
He plowed the fields and planted seeds during the day
Fed the hogs and the chickens

Picked the cotton in the hot sun
All while he thought of his hot lady love

Granny hid his pants in the loft to keep him
From going to his lady love's bed down the road
But papa had spare trousers that he wore most nights
As he walked quickly down the road
To his hot…hot…lady love

Cell Block #20

Mama has a brand new home
Once beautiful....now sad and down
Thick, healthy black hair now white, limp and straggly
Cause she was caught sniffing the white powder
Into her beautiful nose and sticking the nasty
used needles in her arms, hips, and belly
Making her sleep a lot, forgetful and not want
to cook or clean her body or the house
Mama has a brand new home
Who will rock me to sleep at night? Give me my bath?
Cook my food? Hug and kiss me? Now I'm sad, scared,
cry a lot, don't feel good about myself, bitter, resentful
I keep to myself, feel real down, no joy, no happiness
I want to run away and hide
cause
Mama has a brand new home
Did I do something wrong?
I'm angry and confused all the time and other children make fun of me
Cause mama's gone to a new home
Her new address is Cell Block #20

Foster Child

I ain't got no family
I ain't got no home
I ain't got no hugs and kisses
I ain't got no claps and hurrahs
I ain't got no self esteem

I pretend a lot…I dream a lot
I laugh when I'm crying inside
I'm not good enough
I'm moved from place to place
I'm a Foster Child

No More Strength

I've been beat up, tied up, stepped on,
Burned, drugged, cursed, misused, and abused
Now..........
I welcome the big box
Covered with cold black dirt
Topped with beautiful flowers
Cause.........
I'm so tired

My shelter and My Hat

You my love, my protector, shields me for the sun, rain, cold
My protector… lovely in all colors, shapes and form
Soft, floppy and curvy
Zigzag, flowers, stripes
Wool, silk, denim, leather, cotton
My beautiful, perfect hat, my love
My shelter

Once Upon a Time

The fire once burned brightly and hot
Glowed all night – made me warm and fuzzy
Sparkles jumping in my heart and head
And body burning with desire

The once hard "poke" now soft
like smothered coals
The fire is out and no more magic
Once upon a time there was fire and desire
Once upon a time there was love, love, love
Once upon a time…but no more

Drivers

Have you ever watched drivers of cars and trucks
They clean their nose, pick in their ears, comb their hair,
Put on makeup, read the paper, write on paper
Talk on the phone, text, eat and drink, hit and argue
Site see, wave, blow at other drivers, road rage
Lots of drama in moving vehicles

Loneliness

My eyes are wet all night
My body is curled up like a ball
The sounds of night rodents fill my ears
As I jump at their scratches and bumps
I burn inside and out
As I make it through another, sleepless night
I'm so lonely, I hurt all over
I'm just a tired, empty, lonely woman

Staying Focused in the Grocery Store

Anticipating a quick trip to the grocery store
for milk, juice, eggs and cereal
I entered quickly and headed for the milk when my eyes spotted a
big sale on thin pork chops and fresh chicken wings that I could
just taste when seasoned and fried in the piping hot vegetable oil
Then I caught a glimpse of those soft sweet delicious
Hawaiian rolls to wrap around the crisp fried chicken
I took a few more steps and found the big white potatoes, pickled salad
cubes, mayonnaise and eggs needed to fix a delicious bowl of potato
Salad to eat with the wings
I remembered that baked beans go hand in hand with potato salad
Walking to another aisle I picked up some chips and dip,
graham crackers, peanut butter, and a jar of grape jelly
Then my eyes fell on the freezer full of delicious boxes of ice cream…
So many flavors, so many sizes. I grabbed two cartons before
I changed my mind. What's a meal without dessert?
With my basket loaded, I headed towards the cash register
to check out when I remembered that I needed biscuits,
a can of Salmon, syrup and rice for breakfast
I walked quickly to my car and started the ignition to leave then I
remembered the milk, juice and cereal that I came to the store to buy,
but forgot them all as my eyes spotted so many other delicious items.
I need to stay focused in the grocery

Tears of a Clown

Clowns pretend to be lighthearted, happy and funny
Do tricks to entertain the crowds
I make others laugh when I'm crying inside
I use actions…twisting, twirling instead of talking
I have my own special face
I hide behind the thick paint on my face
Bright colors around my sad eyes and crooked mouth
Red eyebrows and large red nose and a
Head of wild yellow hair
I wear bright patched clothes that make me look like
I'm homeless and down on my luck
Tears of a clown are private
Because I can't let you see my face,
My true self, the inner me
You never see my tears cause I cry inside
while wearing thick makeup and
A wide grin on my face

A Servant's Heart

Loving and giving
Encouragement and praise
Kindness to those who crossed her path
Sharing God's promise of spiritual abundance
Believed that we are saved by Grace
Tenderhearted and forgiving heart
A completely humble, patient and gentle spirit
A servant's heart
Yes, Anna Lee, my mama
…the best mama ever

Po Babe

Eyes big, bulging and wild
Deep tracks of tears stain her face
Face distorted like lines drawn on paper
Skin like sand paper
Ears filled with balls of wax

Feet moving slowly
Always the last in line
Looking lost and out of place
Trembling hands with dirty nails
Water running down her legs
when she could not find the potty
or the outhouse

Legs forced open by ruthless boys and men
Filling her with their fiery milk
And then her stomach bloated with a beating heart
Tiny head, feet and hands who came out looking
And acting just like a little Po Babe

Family is....

Hope when you feel hopeless
Calming when the storms of life are raging
Triple A when your car breaks down
Assistance when you feel helpless
Loving when you want affection
Supportive when you lose your job
Stingy when you can't stick to a budget
Freedom when you are incarcerated
A listening ear when you need emotional support
There with you when your child is sick
In grief when death occurs
Comfort when you are lonely
On your side when your partner is unfaithful
A refuge when your house burns down
A cab when you can't drive anymore
A guiding light when you lose your vision
A prosthetic when your legs are amputated
Your rehab when you have heart surgery
Joy and happiness when you live in a nursing home
Irreplaceable when you learn that you have a terminal illness
A home cooked meal when you are hungry
Prayer warriors when you need prayer
Confidence when self-esteem is low
Unconditional love
Collective problem-solving
There for you throughout crisis after crisis after crisis
Family Is L-O-V-E!!
And Family Is...Never Dull!!

"I know a place"

I know a place,
where respect meets professionalism,
where empathy meets consciousness and
where smiles meet tired and sad faces,

I know a place,
where hope is churned out with arm rotations,
legs moving, warm ups and cool downs.

I know a place,
that's clean and safe,
where injured hearts are strengthened by
loving and tender hands.

I know a place,
where there is no gender, no religion, no race …. Just hearts.

Yes, I know a place…. They call it **Cardiac Rehab.**
But, I call it **HOPE!**

"Black Gal"

Black Gal
My black sister didn't have much fun cause
she was known as Black Gal.
My black sister with the shapely charcoal body was
beautiful as the sky at night, bright black eyes, soft
beautiful black skin and thick black hair.
But she was called **Black Gal** so much that she
thought her beautiful black body was ugly.
Black gal, black gal, hold your beautiful black head up!
You are so beautiful to me
Black and beautiful

Black Music

Black music makes me want to be loved and to love some more,
Makes my tears drop to my toes as the sad songs talk of lost love,
and relationships, cheating, wanting several lovers, loneliness,
Sunday morning love and feeling like wasted sugar on the floor.
Black music makes me want to have a lover good or bad … but,
to have one makes me squirm and want to be held so tight.

Beautiful and Sad

A sad, beautiful, talented soul
who sings so often of broken relationships.
She touched the core of my soul as she sang about feeling like
sugar on the floor; I rather go blind than to see you go and
church bells ringing as the man she loved married someone else.
Her deep, deep sadness showed as she sang in an
emotional pitched sad voice about being mistreated,
abused, and left alone and how hard it is
to let go of a man that she loved but did NOT love her back.
Sounds like me and you and so many of us.

Daddy's Truck

Daddy had a big ole truck that he drove from here to there
all day and some of the night.
He didn't need anything since he had a toothbrush,
toothpaste, soap, paper towels, lotion, keys, screws,
papers, receipts, food and more in his truck
He had so much that there was no room for a passenger. The
truck was for him only as he picked up scrap iron, old tires,
and wood that were treasures to him, but junk to others.

Coal Miners

Coal miners with soot on their faces go deep into the
dark, dark, dirty tunnels where the fragile rocks are
ready to fall and tightly squeeze their bodies.
I hope they hugged and kissed their lady love each time they
leave the house and go to the deep, dark, and dirty mine.
Kiss like it is their last kiss

Cracked Egg

My life movie reminds me of a fragile, broken egg cracked by the history of many ups and downs, many broken relationships, lost jobs and more. Sometimes I feel like a fragile cracked egg that cannot be repaired. So I live each minute, each hour waiting … quiet and alone.

The Hat Lady

So many hats I cannot count,
So many colors, shapes and sizes
adorned with roses, stripes, beads, and fancy designs
sitting on top of her head or slightly on the back.
Walking with pride and dignity each Sunday as she sashays
down the aisle to the front of the church knowing that all eyes
are on her, as men admire and women hate with jealousy.

Party Lines

Thank you God for a telephone.
Although it was not a private line but a party line where I
gently picked up the phone, and heard Ms. Jane and her
man friend making plans for a night at the Jukebox motel.
Talking about her husband was out of town and they
could spend the night together for old times sake.
The party line gives me so much ammunition; I could
make a mint from blackmailing the talkers who let their
hearts take over and common sense go by the wayside.

Hands

They come in all sizes, colors, scars and textures and are all good
to have, They look beautiful adorned with diamond rings,
They cook, mend, wash, and bathe.
They give and give to others with no complaints,
They reach out to give love and be loved.
They pulled weeds and picked cotton, cut wood and mowed the yard.
They brought babies into the world, tended to the sick and shut in
with love and food. They cleaned toilets and scrubbed the floors at
the white folks houses. These hands are tired, raw, tattered, wrinkled
and crooked like balled up brown paper, but I love them anyway.

The Big "C"

Cancerous cells throughout my breast,
balled up in my stomach,
limiting breathing in my lungs, deeply embedded
throughout my liver, my colon, and in my pancreas.
My cancerous bones are fragile and painful with limited walking
And many falls
Cancers throughout my body
Spreading all over my body, throughout my blood lines
Chemo, radiation and surgeries
Multiple medications, hair loss, and skin lesions
Keeping me weak, in pain and hopeless as I wait eagerly for the
Pain to end and I will gladly meet my maker when I'm called

The Middle Child

The oldest child is like a valuable showpiece,
proudly introduced to the world, adorned with beautiful clothes and
jewels. The youngest child is spoiled, pampered, over protected, kept
close by …but, the middle child is ignored and left to fend for self.

A Social Worker's Prayer

Lord
As I answer the despairing cry of my clients, help
me to be patient, kind and wise. Give me the
knowledge, strength of spirit, fortitude and
desire to go beyond the expected.
Order my steps.
Let me view their problems from every angle and
through your discerning eyes.
Direct me Lord in all that I do.
Let me not be blinded or sidetracked by the nature of
the problem, the cleanliness of the garb, their lack of strength
and resilience, their negative attitude, their lowness of spirit,
their sense of powerlessness or their financial status.
Let me value the person…every living creature
The downcast, depressed, discouraged, dispirited, defeated
Give me the strength of mind to continue to help
Keep me sensible, dignified, ethical and thoughtful.
Help me to show a pattern of good works in all I do.
I want to help as you help and Love as you Love.
I want to be like you because you are the ultimate
source…
You are the Great, Great, Great Social Worker

The Bus Stop

Black like my mama
Many women stand at the bus stop
with scarves on their head.
No lipstick, powder or rouge
A worn work dress or skirt and blouse, comfortable work shoes
and an old pocketbook as they all … step on the bus and drop
coins in the slot transferred three or four more stops as they
changed buses each time before reaching the white lady's house.
At the white lady's house dressed in an apron and soft
shoes, mama began to sweep, mop, and scrub floors, clean
toilets, wash clothes, clean stoves and refrigerators.
At the end of the day she was given $10.00 and some
left over food for her work as she raced back to the
bus stop, made transfers and returned home.

Sisterly Love

So different in body and mind
One caramel, the other vanilla
Both beautiful in body and spirit
Hugging each other, laughing, running, fighting and playing
Youthful, endless energy
Loving sweets and meats, but hating veggies
Talented, awesome, loving, kind, smart
God's gifts
I call them Skeeter and Pookie

Back in the Day

Baby Ruth, big time, butter finger (5 Cents), Mary Jane
peanut butter kisses and big moon cookies (1 cent),
Sodas sold in bottles,
45 RPM and 33 RPM vinyl records,
clothes lines outside instead of electric dryers,
black iron stoves instead of electric, candles instead of electric lights,
iron heated in fireplace, outdoor toilets, slop jars in the house,
bathing in tin tubs one after another in the same water.
Smoke houses to keep meat fresh in salt boxes,
Movies were 25 cents,
One room schools with all ages taught together,
Large blocks of ice instead of ice from freezer (50 cents),
Party lines for telephones,
Cotton picked by hand.. NO machines,
Fresh chicken from the yard and fresh eggs from the chicken,
Starch for clothes made with flour
No running water,
Sprinkled clothes by hand with water (before ironing),
Chicken backs (per pound 10 cents),
Possums, squirrels and rabbits cooked in gravy.
Yes, I remember these things back in the day.
The Good and the Bad!

Pride And Joy

Let the bells ring loud and clear
The trombones and drums beat loudly in our ears
Let the trumpets announce and salute a true leader
for the diverse people in our country
Let the smiling dancing girls with the wide colorful
ruffled skirts twist and turn to the music
Let the children of all ages clap their hands and stomp their feet
and let the old men and women with teary eyes look to the sky and
rejoice with loud chants of thanks to our heavenly father that we are
given a leader who is committed to reaffirming the sweat, labor and
dedication of men and women who helped make our country great.
New hope that our sons and daughters can be leaders of this
great country and that our brown children can be Presidents,
kings, queens, diplomats and more. A testimony that little brown
children can be proud of their heritage and beautiful brown skin.
Proud of a leader who is professional in attire and behavior, has a
charismatic speaking ability, intelligent, respectful, loves our country
and the diverse populations residing throughout our country.
He is a leader who demonstrates love and dedication to
his family. Respectful and devoted to his little brown girls
and beautiful, intelligent, and charming brown wife.
Still celebrating and cheering with pride at home and abroad
the ethical, courageous leader President Barack Obama #44
Our historical pride and joy

Pole Dancer

Twisting and curling my naked body around
the tall standing iron poles
All eyes focused on me as I crawl slowly up the pole
and slide down at the beat of the sensuous music
I don't mind their piercing eyes and dirty sweaty hands reaching for
me and touching me as they fill my bucket with the green stuff

The Baptism Pool

The long white soft flannel gown
Warm to my touch
The little white cap covered my hair
No makeup, lipstick
No perfume and sweet lotions
No earrings and necklace
To the deep wide pool I slowly walked
Bare feet and scared
To meet the waiting outstretched preacher man's
Waiting arms and then lowered into the cold water
As mama and all the church folks in unison with
Tears rolling down their faces said …
Amen and Amen

Compassion

Eyes, mind and heart that turn away from the sad and hurting

From the broken, demented, homeless, abused,
misused, lonely, and bereaved
From people of domestic and foreign lands
From light, brown and dark skins who suffer and are hurting from
injustices, alcohol, drugs, loneliness, bills, and homelessness
But
Today I see the person and their needs
My heart reaches out and feel them, really feel them
Joy overflowing as I find delight in being thoughtful,
understanding and helpful
Putting love into action and making the best of each new day
Sharing my blessings with the underdogs that are hurting
Compassion is in my soul

Family Walk

Holding hands we strolled down the road in our neighborhood
Our minds relaxed, smiling, joking, observing
nature's beautiful flowers and trees
We talked and laughed and laughed some more
Lots of smiles and hellos…some real and
some fake from old and young folks
Black, white, Asian and others
Thinking about the dishes waiting to be washed and
the floors to be swept we walked faster and returned
home with fond memories of our family walk

Treasured Family Member

Tiny, dark brown and white furry coat covered her tiny body
Short legs that sprinted quickly throughout the house
Green glossy eyes that lit up like a Christmas tree
Gingerly shampooed in the big wash tub
Toweled dry with a clean fluffy towel and warm blow dryer
Loud voice that protected us from strangers
Slept in our laps during the day and on our beds at night
Standing like a soldier begging for chicken, pork, or beef
Lots of love for the little bitty dog
A treasured family member
Coco is her name

She is Worthy

She looks like a withered flower
Head bowed down, arms limp
No color in her skin
Hair like a dirty matted mop
No pep in her steps
Yellow, bulging eyes
A mouth that makes no words
She is trampled on, grabbed, pulled and ridiculed
Very insecure
But…. She is a worthy human being

Singing of God's Goodness

In times of joy, distress and grief
I sing songs about God's goodness and mercy
Songs about trusting and obeying him
How he will make a way for me
No one can beat God giving
Amazing Grace
Take my hand precious Lord
Hold to God's unchanging hand during the day and
In the quietness of the night
That he is my caregiver
I sing songs of Thanksgiving for all that God
has done and is still doing in my life
Singing when I'm happy makes me happier, joyful and thankful
Singing is rejoicing and uplifting when I'm
tested by trials and tribulations
Singing is a monumental source of encouragement to move forward
So I continue to depend on God for today and my tomorrows as I
Move along full of gratefulness
My songs comfort me night and day

Self -Recipe for Growth

30 cups of prayers each day
15 cups of joy in each day
20 cups of thanksgiving for each new day
10 cups of confidence in my ability
 5 cups of strength to explore possibilities
 3 cups of appreciation for my accomplishments
20 cups of positive thoughts
 5 cups of cans and no cannots
 6 cups of facing challenges
 7 cups of no fixed limitations
 5 cups of no pessimistic thoughts
 4 cups of patience
10 cups of service to others
10 cups of forgiveness
10 cups of love for others
11 cups of seeking opportunities for growth
    This is my recipe for self growth

Mama's Bible

Worn, torn, faded and fragile from days and nights of
Turning pages to find scriptures and write personal notes
Pages folded from years of reading God's instructions for our lives
Forgiveness of our sins and forgiveness of those who hurt us
Worn from turning pages again and again to read of
God's amazing grace and everlasting mercies
Pages tattered, torn and stained from flipping pages
and tears falling on the pages when reading of
God's new mercies and miracles each day
Creases deep from folding on special examples
of Christian commitment,
The fruits of the spirit, God's providential care
Mama's bible has lots of history
Birthdays, deaths, anniversaries, graduations,
baptisms and other important milestones
Though torn, worn, faded, wrinkled, dirty, fragile and used
I love my mama's Bible

A Father's Love

An example of Love for God
A good listener
Supportive and present when needed
A true model of respectfulness, kindness, patience, leadership
Encouraging children to reach their potential
Guiding hand
A strong work ethic
Dedication to family
Selfless caring
Gives praise
A shoulder to lean on
Provides words of wisdom
A commitment to provide for his family
Provides insight into problems, people, and situations
Always there for his children and showing
them how to love and live life
Teaches his children to accept life's challenges and use them to grow
Commitment to the emotional, moral and
social development of his children

Unlovable

My skin is beautiful and I am adorned in my silk,
waiting for a tender hot look in your eyes
and magical fire radiating throughout my body
But… like the trees in the bitter cold of winter
I lay
naked, unwanted,unfulfilled, and lacking full beauty
My heart and body hurt
cause I am not loved

Trick or Treat

Children in groups running from door to door throughout the neighborhood
Mothers and fathers close behind them
Dressed in beautiful costumes, paint on their faces and decorations on their heads
Some dressed as lady bugs, mermaids, Princess, black cats with orange eyes, witches, cowboys, superman, superwoman and more
Baskets or buckets in their hands waiting for the mouthwatering treats
Lots of smiles, lots of treats dropped in the baskets
No tricks for the generous givers, just smiles and thanks.

My Folks

Born and raised in the deep south, the Mississippi Delta
Water poured out of the bodies of men, women and
children who bent down all day in the blazing sun
picking the white balls from their low bushes
picking and canning the butter beans green beans,
squash,okra watermelons, sweet potatoes, collard and
turnip greens to store away for the winter
cutting wood for the big black iron stove and fireplaces
for the winter cold
living in little wooden houses sprinkled far apart
where hours were spent sitting on the porch
gazing at the sky and the land,
when all folks sat quietly or laid on the floor during the
fierce, sharp lightning and loud thunder storms
spent hours sitting with the sick
rode in the wagon or truck to the little wooden
church to thank God for his mercy
weekly trip to town on Saturday to buy
things that were not made at home
eating squirrels, rabbits, and fresh chicken from the yard
collecting fresh eggs for cakes and cornbread

Wow! I love my Mississippi folks

Footprints of a Good Man

A good man loves God
Is forgiving
Is tenderhearted
Is kind
Is slow to anger
Is not bitter
Is not deceitful
Is not jealous
Has no rage
Does not hate others
Is not envious
Is patient
A good man surrenders his heart to God
will do charitable deeds in private
Shows mercy and compassion
Is honest
will not steal
Will walk in love
Loves his family
Is a role model for his children
Encourages others

My Prayer Room

Sometimes my bad days out number my good days
They are sometimes filled with impossible
challenges and giant obstacles
So much backbiting, lying and cheating
Then I go into my tiny space in my closet and sit on a soft wide cloth
to feel the presence of the Lord
My space has a feeling of awesomeness and
majestic magic and calmness
I am showered with calmness like a fresh rain and quietness
as I communicate with the my heavenly father
I feel the serenity, peace, and quietness
As I focus on yesterday, today, and tomorrow and as I think
about the many memories of blessings in the past and to come
There are no glass windows in my prayer room to steal my attention
Helping me to stay focused and look at my challenges
from different angles and new and different perspectives
Giving me strength to keep going. I love
my sanctuary, my prayer room
We all need a Prayer Room
I

Church Folks

Brown, Black, and White bodies
Baptists, Catholics, Methodists, non-denomination
Old, young and babies
Rich, poor and in between
Big hats, little hats, no hats
Old dresses, new dresses
Tight dresses, long dresses, short dresses
Pants tight….pants sagging
Piano playing, organ playing, drums beating
Singing songs about God's grace and mercy
A shelter in the time of storm
The Lord will make a way somehow
Hold to God's unchanging hands
Clapping and waving their hands and arms
Smiles and no smiles
Some coughing, some sleeping, some crying, some quiet
Some talking, some chewing, some singing
All of these while sitting on the church pews
Church folks…

Dreams

Loudly calling strange names
Twisting from side to side
Legs up and down
Sweat popping even on a cold night
Breathing hard and loud grunting noise
Snot running down my face
As I'm beaten, stomped and chased
Heart pumping wildly as my eyes open to a new day
I can't get up because I'm completely wasted from
Fighting and scratching, kicking and running in my dreams.

The Broken Drum

I am broken and can't make beautiful music
No one can hear my joyful sounds
I've been mended and patched and patched again
But I still can't make no music
My heart flickers rapidly with hard times
and more hard times
No fire, no magic, no smiles, no laughter
I can't make music

Useless

My beautiful skin is soft to the touch and flawless
I'm adorned in my expensive pearls
my silk dress and my sequined high heel shoes
Waiting for tender hot love in your eyes
and magical fire throughout my body
I wait and wait and wait some more
But…like a tree naked in the bitter cold of a winter
ice storm, I stand frozen like an iron statue
All around me are soaked, frozen, brown leaves matted together
and lay naked, unwanted, unfulfilled, and lacking full beauty.
My heart and my body hurt cause I'm beautiful,
but unloved and useless like the naked tree

Strong

I too stand tall like the deeply fertilized Oak tree
Strong limbs and deep roots
Richly covered with healthy, green leaves
Tall, strong and proud with out stretched arms
When I eat, sleep, work, play and love
I'm content…I'm fulfilled …I'm strong
Like
The oak tree

The Deep South

Down in the deep, deep south, My folks
Lived in tiny, wooden houses with tin roofs and wooden floors
Red hard clay dirt yards swept clean during the summer.
Houses sprinkled far apart
Outhouse as a toilet and night slop jar in the house
Water from the deep wells… no running water
Used flour mixed with water for starching clothes
Horses, pigs, hogs, squirrels, chickens were family

Picked cotton for the white man in the summer heat
Cooked and canned beans, squash, okra, collards,
sweet potatoes, tomatoes, peanuts and more
Meat stored in the smokehouse for winter months
Made ice cream with block ice and hand cranked buckets
Wood gathered for winter heat and cooking
Hot bricks used to heat the beds

Sat on the porch and talked for entertainment
Gazed at the stars and moon way into the night hours
Horses and trucks were used for transportation
to the nearby town for shopping
Cooked and sat with the sick for hours and hours
Sat quietly during storms cause "the Lord was working"
Prayer warriors
My Mississippi Folks are awesome.

Round-up

Daddy is a good man
Works 9 to 5 and takes good care of us
He plays with mama and gives her lots of hugs and kisses
Teaches me how to play basketball and ride my bike
Daddy went to work today but didn't return home
Stopped by some men in uniforms and sent back to a far away land
Mama's tears ran down her face
She now sits quietly for hours staring through the window
Hoping daddy will walk through the door
Depression and sadness in her teary eyes cause
daddy's gone and can't come back
No more hugs and kisses goodnight
No more running, jumping and playing with me
No daddy in our house to make us feel safe and secure
During sleepless nights I ask the question why
Why? Why? Why?
Why my family can't stay together in this beautiful
home of the brave and land of the free

Grief

Head bowed low
No singing heart—no laughter
Tempers flaring
Sleepless red eyes dripping like waterfalls
Face swollen and shoulders drooping
Mouth twisted in sorrow
Nails dirty
Clothes tattered and torn
Faith diminished
Sounds like you and me…full of grief

Hard Times

I haven't seen you for a long, long time
Where have you been hiding?
I wanted to tell you about my hard times
Did you hear...
that I lost my job?
that my house burned down?
that I had no place to sleep?
that my car stopped running
that my man left me and the kids
That my son is strung out on the white powder and long dirty needles?
That I turned to liquor, pills and cocaine to help me forget
Where are you?
Where are you, my friend?
I need you...cause I'm having hard times.

Daddy's New Baby

Belly swollen and about to pop
Never leaving the house
School…a distant memory
Hands stretched out for pennies or dollars
While her daddy is looking puzzled, scared, quiet and guilty
Cause his daughter is carrying a seed…his seed
Daddy's having a brand new baby

Compassion

Eyes and mind and heart that turn away from those that are:
Sad and hurting, broken, demented, homeless,
abused, misused, lonely, bereaved
From: people of domestic and foreign lands
From: light, brown and dark skins who suffer
and are hurting from injustices, alcohol, drugs,
loneliness, bills, homelessness and cell blocks.

Today, I see the person and the Needs
My heart reaches out and feels them
Joy is overflowing as I find delight in being thoughtful,
understanding and helpful by putting love into actions
Making the best of each new day and
Sharing my blessings with those that are hurting
Compassion is in my soul
Compassion runs deep in my soul.

The Graveyard

All people…young and old
From domestic and foreign lands
All nationalities
The educated and uneducated
The demented
The gifted
Movie stars, politicians, preachers
From the poor house to the white house
Lie still in the dark boxes
In the cold black dirt
There is quietness and serenity as passer byers
look and look and look some more
As memories dance in their heads

The Big House

The big brick house with brown bricks, white trim and
large white columns—big rooms and small rooms
Wooden floors, ceramic floors, and floors
covered with thick luxury carpet
A spotless white kitchen
Four spacious, relaxing bathrooms with big tubs and showers
and roomy closets with food galore and lots of laughter
Oh… but this is your house. Not mine.

The Cemetery

A quiet, quiet place filled with beautiful flowers, flags,
headstones and special what-nots laid gingerly on each
layer of stone that covers that black, cold dirt.
In the big roomy box buried deep in a hole are red, black,
white, brown bodies of all ages and sizes, dressed in
their "Sunday best" now lie still in the dark box.
Their color, hair, size, and history does not
matter in the big, quiet cemetery

Hustling

Bodies of all colors, sizes and nationalities
Eyes dazed and spacy
Eyebrows and eyelids caked with black tar
Lips popping with shiny, red paint and big,
wide hoops adorning their ears

Fake gold necklaces and bracelets
Mini dresses and no panties
Ashy legs and high, high heel shoes
Looking for the green bills from dirty, young, old, tainted bodies
All colors and nationalities
With pockets full of green paper
Although filthy and dirty I want you anyway
cause…
I need to pay my rent and buy food to feed my hungry kids.

Pole Dancer

Twisting and curling my naked body around the tall iron poles
The loud sensual music relaxes my mind
and body as I move to each beat
All eyes are focused on me
as I crawl up the pole
with legs closed and then opened wide
as I slide down
and move to the beat of the music.
I don't mind their piercing and admiring eyes.
I don't mind the touch of their dirty, sweaty hands
when they fill my panties with the green stuff.

The Mailbox

The little tin box
Filled with steals and deals
From folks trying to sell
Their wares and make a lot
Of the green bills
Too many deals that are not real
Like quick and delicious meals
Latest trends in what to wear
Beauty tips and buys that cost too much
Telling us how to shave and soften oily skin
Books to read to grow the mind
Cleaning products that I can't buy
Simple diets to make us happy
Colorful rugs that can't be walked on
Quick techniques to tackle our goals
Crafts that cost too much
Ways to tighten the tush
Bills I can't pay
Charities pleading for the disabled, needy and sick
Sending name labels and 5 cent and 10 cent coins to get me
To send them some green backs
All in my mailbox, but going into my trash box.

My Chair

So many fannies, dry, wet and soiled sit in
my worn, tired, peaceful chair
Quiet as midnight when all critters are sleeping
My chair inhales different odors from different
bodies, actions and experiences
Discolored, dirty, funky and sagging…
my chair stands strong
I return again and again, feeling good and welcome
in the alluring, soothing,
welcoming and warm arms of my chair…
waiting patiently to hear and feel my thoughts,
my love and my deep pain.

What About Me?

Your laws protect women, minorities, veterans and the
physically and mentally handicapped from
discrimination in housing, public places and employment
I get no pension, no social security, no inheritance, no
veterans benefits, no health care, nothing......
Because of this, I hide who I am and who I love
I hide my affection and my love in public
I hide my love for my wonderful, faithful partner
Because we are together.....we get no presents,
no congratulations, no encouragement
No preferential treatment for us
No priviledges for us
Cause.....
We are gay and lesbian Americans
What about me?
What about us?

I Look The Part

I have blue eyes, pale white skin, thin nose
Long black, brown, blonde hair
I am equality, justice and freedom
I receive many, many benefits when
I enter a store to shop
apply for a job
walk into a bank
apply for a scholarship
wave down a cab
apply for a mortgage loan
Interview for an Ivy League school
Yes, I fit in perfectly because I look the part

I work hard to keep the beautiful red, white and blue Confederate flag
That honors my heritage
I can't help it if other folks suffer daily from
discrimination, abuse and economic oppression

I am young…I have never committed any injustices against people of
Color
But…. I enjoy the privileges that I have…..
because of past and present discrimination
I'm so thankful that I look the part.
Yes, I look the part…I'm privileged…yes, very privileged

I Need You

Daddy, I need you
To be active, present, and loving in my life
To love, nurture and protect me
To teach me how to be a man...a responsible man

I need you..
To support and guide me
To help me lead a healthy, caring and productive life
To help me stay away from the white powder and poisonous needles
To keep me from being a criminal and
making my home in a cell block

I need you although I know that you can't hold a job cause you
sniff the white powder, use the poisonous needle filled with
drugs, drink white lightening and act real wild like a fool
I know you are thin as a rail and sickly.......
throwing up day and night
But..... I need you
I know you didn't love mama and you didn't like to
be married but, don't turn your heart from me

Daddy, daddy, where are you? I need you in my life
Get your mind and body together
Cause I really, really need YOU

I Am A Woman

Devalued in my home, at my job and in my culture
Powerless and loss of voice in a man's world
Exploited in the work place and relationships
Deprived of status, wants, needs, capabilities, dreams and worth
Abused in relationships
Choices hindered by laws
Oppression from years of stereotyping and cultural domination
Please hear my cry, my voice, so loud..
so often during the day and all night
Empower me..
Recognize my worth…
I am somebody, I am valuable, I am hopeful,
I refuse to give up, I matter
I am a woman…. I am a woman day and night

Privileged

I creep around in the dark at the Ace Motel and the Do Drop Inn
Swaying and staggering with a belly full of
Morgan David and Jack Daniel
My eyes wide open and eying the glitter covered dark brown
curvy body and her red lips and then the white pale body
with a tight, tight skirt, no panties, no bra and then.....
another little shapely Asian wearing nothing under the
colorful moomoo. Three in one night I'm feeling lucky
and quite fulfilled and satisfied as I tasted each one
But, don't judge me cause
I'm not a whore, I'm not a freak. I'm a man. I'm privileged

Once Up .... Now Down

For so many moons we were divided....
The haves and have nots
The good and the bad
The moral and immoral
Some living like kings and Queens
With money in the bank, stock, bonds and land
Many had no compassion, not courteous,
not tenderhearted and not humble
Others like peons with zero assets living from day to day
Needing help to exist
Then... there were no more haves and have nots when the
stock market crashed and the money once plentiful was
lost. We were all in the same boat. It was us. It was we.
We were once up....now down because of
the spirit of the Great Depression.
Once up......but now down

Why Do You Love Me?

Is it my smile
The dimples in my cheeks
The twist of my hips
My sweet sugar lips
The longing in my eyes
The soft touch of my hands
My positive attitude
My lingering kiss

Is it because of the way I make you feel
My love for you shines brightly
Because I'm a keeper
Because I protect you
Because I respect you
Because everyday is something new
My love for God
Tell me….tell me…..tell me
Why do you love me?
Whatever it is…Keep on loving me

Repulsion

Don't look at me like that!
Don't frown at me like that!
You call me crazy and sinful
You call me wicked and sick
My name is Sam
Yes, my name is Sam
Don't hate me because I love Bill
Don't pity me because I was born this way
Don't pity me

Love me, support me, accept me, appreciate me
Cause I'm a real person
Cause I'm different
I was born this way

I'll Think of You

When the sun rise each new day and show it's beautiful
bright face and the Moon show its quiet beauty at night
I'll think of you
When the butterflies kiss the flowers and the birds
sing as they rest on the branches of the trees
I'll think of you
When the seasons change…Spring and summer flowers
salute the sun and trees wear their deep green leafy coats…
then Fall, when the trees shed their leaves like raindrops, and
winter's beautiful white blanket of snow covers the ground
I'll think of you
When I hear children's voices full of excitement on
the playground and in the neighborhood
I'll think of you
When I see little girls jumping rope, playing tag and hide and seek
I'll think of you
When I see little dresses and beautiful bows and ribbons
I'll think of you
When I see girls dressed for Debutante balls and high school proms
I'll think of you
When I see puffy clouds like marshmallows in the sky
and know that you are in God's loving arms
I'll think of you
Yes, I will always think of you and always love you
My Angel

Regrets

I look like deep brown and green beaten and crushed leaves
Swallow me today and tomorrow and you'll
want me and yearn for me everyday
You'll want more and more and more of me because I
make you feel so rested and calm all day and night
I make you so bold and giddy ..jolly and carefree
I make you feel like you are dancing like a pro
But, later I won't let you make decisions,
remember people, facts or things
Your attention span is short
You're grouchy and short tempered
You begin to hear loud and soft voices talking to and about you
Paranoia sets in and affect your interactions
Once blue collar, now no collar
Many days I know you regret kissing, tasting, eating and loving me
Yes, you regret meeting ME…but you love ME
My name is weed, pot or marijane

The Nursing Home

Dressed in their saggy pants, big shirts and slippers, they
walk gingerly down the hall or roll their wheelchairs
Food sticking to their faces, neck, and hands
Their laps catching all that dribble and fall
When I look at them, I see loss and hurt in their spacey far away eyes
I see loneliness and hopelessness
I see loss of mobility, loss of strength, and loss of desire
Some have missing limbs, little, few or no teeth, no speech,
humped shoulders, oxygen pipes running through their nose,
pants rolled up, shoes with holes, heavy sweaters, tee
shirts, wheelchairs, walking canes, and walkers
Still others are yawning, heads bowed, eyes lowered, hands
trembling, legs shaking…just sitting for hours and passing time
Still others on guerneys…Many are
overweight and others thin as a rail
All of them waiting for the day and time when they will
leave the nursing home and meet their heavenly father.

Solitude

Smiling sunflowers in the field
Trees standing still as the wind whispers
When the rain falls softly and covers the grass
When stomachs are full and satisfied
When butterflies kiss and taste the flowers
When hawks, coyotes, crickets, owls, dogs,
and cats sleep soundly at night
When there are no bills in the mailbox
When voices are sweet and soft and
When there's no swearing, no screaming, and no evil eyes
I love Solitude

The New Me

I am tired and burned out
Angry, irritable, and short tempered
I now doubt myself, feel anxious, helpless,
No joy and no happiness
I am spiritually low, have poor judgement and introspection
I'm still working, but can't work productively without joy and hope
I am working hard to find the NEW ME..
The strength to endure,
to be grateful, kind, hopeful, loving, giving and
industrious and to be a solid rock
Yes, a solid rock….the NEW ME

The Trauma Conference

Males, females, young, middle age and old
White, Black, Asian, Indian
Brown hair, blonde hair, gray hair, black hair, red hair
Long, short, medium,
Ponytails, balls, braids, curls, straight, natural,
Wearing clothes of varied types and colors
Some sleeping, nodding, reading, talking, eating
Others attentive with awe and anticipation
Still others amazed and deeply saddened
by the nature of daily traumas
And their everlasting physical and mental impact.
Devastating Traumas in Life are displayed and discussed at the
Trauma Conference

If Keys Could Talk

So many keys…..big and small
New, old, rusty
Opens good, private and forbidden doors
If keys could talk…they would tell
My life story….the good, the bad, the ugly
Some I'd like to keep and others I want to forget.

Resilience

Resilience is needed to live well and to succeed
Resilience is needed to keep disappointments, anger in check
And exhaustion from derailing my best plans
To overcome my setbacks and unexpected twists and turns
And strong winds of life
Resilience is needed to buffer rocks thrown in my path to success
I need it, but I don't have it

Real Love

You were never touched by fear
You were never cold....never hungry
Never alone and most importantly you
Knew the tenderness of love
The giving nature of love and
the give and take of real love.

I'll Be Good

I'll be good today
I'll behave tomorrow
I'm loving and kind and generous
I'm helpful and obedient
I'll make you so proud
If you will let me live with you forever
If you will love me and keep me forever
I'm tired of moving from place to place
I need stability instead of being tossed from home to home
I need a family
I need a permanent home
Give me a chance
Let me show you
I'll be good
I promise

I Still Want You

You've been in and out of jail...
a drug seller and user you are
You've beat and killed others
You've burned my house
You're a cheater and a liar
You're a pimp
You're ungrateful
You've been these things and more but.....
I still love you...I still want you...
You are so important and valuable to me
Stay here with me and I hope you will change
I still love you
I still want you

The Bridge

So many days of feeling tattered and torn
Abused and misused
With salty water in my eyes and tear stains
On my face plus failure in my head that
beats all day like a bass drum
I slowly moved one foot and then another to stand on the edge of the
beautiful bridge that overlooked the deep dark hungry river that
Called my name and welcomed me with open arms as I
moved forward and kissed it and became one of many who
thought that it would be better to join the many devouring
water creatures than to remain a helpless creature.

Old Tree

Once standing tall and strong with pride
Proud of your strength and quiet beauty...Changing
vibrant colors from one season to another
Waving your lovely arms as the wind blows softly
Now wrapped and hugged tightly by grey mold and decay
Black soot smeared all over your body
Hungry bag worms feast on your body until your head and
once strong arms are bending like an old, old man waiting
anxiously to meet his maker

Black

Black in my Advocacy
Proud of where I have been and where I am going
Privileged to be part of a rich history of people
Debutante
College Graduate
Sorority Member
Inherited Assets
Leader in Church
Management Position
Good Insurance
Home Paid For
Car Paid For
I'm all this and more,
I'm black, proud and privileged

Toxic

I love the aroma and feeling I get from my pot
Even love the aroma of a room full of this
powerful scent sashaying up my nostrils
As the rich deep odor overwhelms me and tickles my nose I feel it
in my head and my stomach and I continue to partake although ...
my tummy is huge with a beautiful baby ready to enter my world
I forgot about my tiny precious jewel as I continue to enjoy the aroma.
The next day, my bundle of joy entered my world with high
pitched screams, short stubby arms and legs, a damaged heart,
weighing almost two pounds and shaking like a leaf.
Finally, it was clear that the deep satisfying aroma was toxic on
my tiny bundle of joy....the aroma had deep, dark lasting effects

Deception

I look like crushed leaves, deep brown and green
Swallow me today and tomorrow and you'll
want more and more of me
I make you feel good all day and night although
later you can't tell night from day
Can't make decisions
Won't let you remember today or yesterday
Can't pay attention to anything
Grouchy and short tempered
Seeing and hearing voices
Paranoid
Can't hold a job
Many days and nights I know you regret kissing,tasting, eating, and
Loving me.

Affirmations

I see beauty, goodness, calm instead of chaos,
love not hatred
Peace instead of fighting
Togetherness instead of division
I see healing, challenges, opportunities to be creative
Times to bridle my tongue
I see daily grace and am thankful
I see unexpected resources
I see connections, support and positive relationships
I see fulfillment

I see light despite darkness of some days
I see hope overshadow thoughts of despair
I am grateful when the sun rise each new day
And
God's guiding grace and presence in my life
I See, Therefore I Know

A Leader

Beautiful as a new sunrise
Vibrant as a full bloom sunflower
Deep dark eyes and a head covered with thick black hair
Above her years intellectually as she speak the words of
a twelve year old while she's only three years old
Abounding energy and loving
Jumping from anything high
running, rolling, throwing balls
building creative block buildings
coloring pictures and writing notes to her mom and dad
Playing doctor, cooking at her play stove
Playing dress-up in her favorite princess outfits
Singing and dancing in front of a crowd
Playing hide and seek in the house
Patting little Coco, the tiny dog too hard
Walking through the beautiful Xmas tree forest and playing
with the trains at GG and Granddaddy's house
Pookie...so beautiful, sweet, loving, creative, and daring
Destined to be a creative, competent, kind, ethical, leader
Pookie.... A Leader

A Blessing

When the sun shows its bright face, the puffy clouds
stand out like giant marshmallows against the light blue
sky and the moon stands bright against the dark sky, I
thank God for this beautiful gift called Skeeter
When the rain falls gently from the clouds and
the snow falls like diamonds during the cold brisk
days, I thank God some more for Skeeter, a
blessing with big beautiful black eyes
adorned with thick curly eyelashes
and dark eyebrows, tiny nose and mouth on a smooth caramel face.
Destined to be loved by many and to be a blessing to many others.
Never afraid to express her love with words and deeds…
"I love you to the moon and back"
"I love you one million, trillion, zillion times"
"You're the best GG"
Combing her mom and GG's hair
Rubbing lotion on her GG's tired legs
"I love you granddaddy because you teach me so many things"
So much love…So much genuine and thoughtful deeds
Each new day I see, I express my thanks to God for blessing
us with this beautiful, loving, and thoughtful angel.
I call her Skeeter, a blessing from God.

The Gymnast

What do I want to be when I grow up?
What do I want to be when I grow up?
What can I be?
I have had lots of swimming lessons, dance lessons, and music lessons
Right now I love walking on the balance beam, rolling and tumbling
and doing lots of cartwheels in the house and in the yard
Right now, I want to be a gymnast
Next year, maybe something else
Sydney…the gymnast

Favorite Foods

I want breakfast pizza! Make me some pancakes!
I really want more grits.
Brownies and oatmeal chocolate chip cookies and somores
are my favorite sweet treats
I want hot chocolate…right now…please
I want chicken nuggets from Chick-filet too
Ok…Ok…Ok …Patience is a virtue
I know your favorite foods
my sweet baby …Sage

Dress-Up

Adorned beautifully as Princess Sophia
Another day superwoman, mermaids, pirates, cowgirls,
Still another day as Doctors, nurses, teachers, chefs and
Still another day sunflower, ladybug, or strawberry short cake
Strutting through the house with pride and beauty
as they pretend to be whatever they are dressed as.
So much fun! So much pride! Learning about people, professions
and things for hours and hours and
then wanting to sleep in their chosen
dress-up outfit of the day

Two Little Doctors

Dressed in their little white coats
A stethoscope in their hands
and their little black doctor bag nearby
filled with band aids and thermometers,
they listen to my heartbeat with a serious look
then begin to feel my legs and ankles to check for swelling
and then checked my eyes and ears for infections
while talking to each other and to me about my condition
After examining me thoroughly,
with a serious look,they gave me some instructions
and sent me home. Two little doctors just like
their mommy Lita and Auntee Shammie.

My Daughters

You are…..
Intelligent, beautiful, strong, kind, humble
You are…..
Gifted, resourceful, discerning, courageous, motivators
You have…
Unconditional positive regard for others
A love for family
A love for God

What Does Family Feel Like?

Family feels like…
A security blanket
Unconditional love
Acceptance
Physical safety
Psychologically accepted
Dependable
Sharing chores
Nurturing and caring
Consistent, predictable, enriching care
Supportive
Knowledgeable about available resources
Teaching life skills
Ethical behavior
Hope and love

No Place Like Home

Wall smeared by dirty hands
No food left at each meal
Sharing daily chores
Three or four sleeping in a bed
Cousins, aunts, and uncles living with us until they find jobs
Not sparing the rod when disobedient
A safe, healthy, but crowded environment
Lots of love
No place like home

Thanksgiving

Around the long table with its pretty laced tablecloth we sat
Bowed heads, eyes closed, holding hands
Family, friends and enemies
Giving thanks for all their blessings and then eyeing the
big golden brown Turkey and honey baked ham, potato
salad, mac and cheese, sausage casserole, green beans,
collard greens, potato pies, cakes and other dishes
Together at Thanksgiving

My Soul mate

Happy Birthday to one of my favorite people
Thanks for being here… for being you
I'm so glad you are on this earth
I hope you feel loved and appreciated today,
because you are appreciated everyday
Thanks for being wonderful.
Thanks for being You.
With love that will never stop growing
Oceans of love and gratitude to you my soul mate…Budie
With warmest wishes and love on your birthday and always.

Loveless and Alone

You look at me with wild accusing eyes
Your hands seem reluctant to touch me
and your arms can't stretch enough to reach my weak
frame that reflect multiple parasitic infections.
Your heart lacks compassion as you debate
the reason for my predicament
You stand at a distance as if you will catch what I have
I'm forced to become the silent recluse
Thinking deeply about our loveless past, your intense distaste
and aversion for me and lack of empathy and love
I keep a safe distance while waiting for death to
end this friendless, lonely and loveless life

A Ride in the Yard

My daddy took me for a ride in the yard . I saw....
a big oak tree
a green pine tree
pear, walnut and pecan trees
A blooming dogwood tree with pink flowers
a bush with red roses
Yellow lilies
Squirrels, chipmunks and rabbits running in the yard
Birds in the trees
Butterflies, bumble bees and wasps
A hawk in the tree
Green grass
Thank you Daddy,
I love you and thank you for an exciting ride in the yard

A Thank You Letter to My Social Worker

Dear Ms. Judkins,

I'm writing this letter to thank you, thank you, thank you for being so good to me and my children. Thank you for looking out for me and my children. You kept your ears wide open and listened to all my problems even though you had so many other folks that needed your help. You wiped away my tears when they flowed like the river Jordan. You helped me feel real good about myself when I didn't feel like I was worth a dime. Thank you.. Thank you… thank you…Hallelujah.. I Thank the Lord for you Ms. Judkins.

I really thank you Ms. Judkins for helping me get my children back. You believed me when I told you that I love my children…. All seven of them. Thank you for showing me how to save a few dollars for hard times and for finding us a place to live that didn't have no holes in the ceiling and the roof, no roaches, no rats and no spiders. You are such a good encourager. You are such a good, decent, caring, professional social worker. Thank you, thank you, thank you and thank you some more.

May God bless you and protect you everyday.

Sincerely,

Mrs. Susie Mae Tate and children

Barren

My heart says yes, yes
Yours and mine meet and kiss
and dance like one quiet ecstasy after stormy delight
for we are sure that the result of our intertwine
would be a beautiful soul
Boy or girl … pure delight
Instead…not yet
Again we repeat the magic
time and time again
only to hear … Not yet!!!

Behind Bars and Forgotten

There are millions of us living with the same address
in the same home behind bars
We all have numbers and dress alike
We are male, female, transgendered, bisexual, gay, straight
Black, white, yellow, mixed
Mothers, fathers, uncles, aunts, cousins, grandparents, neighbors
White collar, blue collar, and no collar
Disabled and mentally ill
abused and misused
We trade sex for money, food, drugs and protection
AIDS is the farthest thing from our minds
cause other pressures crowd our minds
We are behind bars and forgotten
Loose bowels keep us close to the pot cause we don't
have a lot of extra orange clothes
Food move through our bodies like a roto rooter,
keeping us slim, lacking nutrients and sickly
AIDS is our reality
We are behind bars and forgotten
New infections often but we continue to mix and
mingle cause we need love….we want love
We mix in the raw cause that's all we have
Who cares about the rubbers?
AIDS is our reality
We are behind bars and forgotten
We are behind bars, tongue tied with AIDS and forgotten

Blocked Red River

Arteries blocked with the hard stuff
Won't let the red river flow
Throughout the streets in my body
The highways and byways loaded and blocked with
freaky hard stuff from sugar, bread, cheese and fat
meats that won't let the red river flow freely
The red river presses hard to break the barriers
but the hard stuff won't let it through
Lots of pressure is given to push the red river
through, making the road real weak
Damage from the pressure, now not safe to travel
Worrying, grief, depression, smoking, won't soften the
hard stuff, but makes it harder for the red river to flow
safely and smoothly through my blocked arteries
Now... my heart is full of deep, stabbing pain

Bruised, Twisted, …
But Not Broken

Toughness
Self- sacrifice
Erosion of self esteem
tension, worry, fear
stress and anxiety
Self last and others first
dragging a heavy weight around
little hope and positivity
Bruised and twisted…
But still not broken

Cans and Cannots

Cans…
…Help me climb trees to see from different angles
the things that I could not see from the ground
…Help me to burn the midnight oil to
achieve the seemingly unachievable
…Help me to be faithful to my mate after years of unfaithfulness
…Help me to do what I never did before
…Help me to be silent when I need to be
and to know how my words affect others

While ….
Cannots..
Prevent me form growing, doing, excelling, seeing, experimenting
and just plain stunts my growth

Saint Nick

My favorite person, Saint Nick is coming tonight
Decked out in his red hat, red suit and black boots
and heavy black sack draped over his shoulder
Bringing gifts for all of us …wool coat and socks for mama, a
new cell phone for daddy, a warm blanket for grandma, a new
doll and pretty dresses for sister and a bicycle and skates for me
He will know my house because each window has beautiful pine trees
Decorated with shining ornaments and tiny bright
lights sprinkled throughout the branches
Red poinsettias lined up the long staircase and festive
pillows and blankets laid neatly on the sofa
The long kitchen table is covered with delicious pies, cakes and fancy
hard and soft candy and sizzling hot cider to wash the sweets down
We love Saint Nick and we love Christmas
We sent lots of Thank you letters to Saint Nick for years and years
until I was 13 years old and I tipped downstairs and saw the man
in the red suit was not really Saint Nick but was my daddy who was
sweaty and tired from wearing the tight red suit and the big heavy sack
filled with bricks and not toys. No more Saint Nick…. He is Daddy

Granny

Hats on her head like a flower garden
Strutting down the long dirt road to the little church
house with the Holy book in her hand
Trailing her were her children and other folk children
to hear the preacher man.
Her smile was like bright sunshine
A servant in helping others
Giving hands and willing heart
Drying tears with her skirt
Feeding and sitting with the sick
Picking cotton and lots of veggies in the hot summer heat
canning food for winter months
Chopping wood to heat the house
Feeding the hogs, milking the cows and churning the butter
You are the strength in me
Now You are resting with our Savior from
all your earthly labor and pain.

Hard Life

My folks were born and raised in the deep
south .. the Mississippi Delta
Water poured out of the bodies of men, women, and
children who bent down all day in the blazing sun
plucking the white balls from their low bushes
picking and canning the butter beans, green beans, squash, okra,
watermelons, sweet potatoes, and greens to store away for the winter
Cutting wood for the big stove and fireplaces for the winter cold
living in little wooden houses sprinkled far apart
where hours were spent sitting on the porch
gazing at the sky and the land
and where folks sat quietly or laid on the floor during
the fierce lightning and thunder storms
Spent hours sitting with the sick, reading the
Bible and rubbing their aching bodies
Rode in the wagon or truck to the little wooden
church to thank God for his mercy
They made a trip to town on Saturday to buy
things that were not made at home
Eating squirrels, rabbits, and chickens from the yard
I love my folks
My Mississippi folks had a hard life but
lots of love for family and others

Hospital Blues

Oxygen flowing
Blood flowing through IV to nourish weak tired lifeless veins
Techs coming and going to check temperature and Blood pressure
and draw more and more blood
from the tired struggling veins
Nurses blow up veins and make arms look like a drug party
IV dripping saline and dangerous antibiotics
Painkillers entering the body to mask the real problems
Reminded to wash hands and don't touch!!
Garlic breath knows no boundaries when
patient and nurse are nose to nose
Privacy unknown as I'm naked and spread
open like the wings of an eagle.

Hungry

I'm so hungry I want to eat
Really want to eat
a big red apple, a long ripe banana, a soft orange
two little grapes, and a juicy yellow pear
On this beautiful day,
I ate….some carrots, beans, tomatoes
some peas, some squash
some sweet potatoes
some mashed potatoes and some fruits
My mom gave me these good vegetables and fruits on
this beautiful day. Please do it tomorrow too.
Thank you mom.

I Fall Short

I did not teach you to pray, give thanks, stand for righteousness,
encourage the helpless, inspire others, and count your blessings.
I Fall Short

I didn't even teach you to give hope, share kindness,
give praise, share joy, show empathy and fight for human rights.

I fall short... I fall short
as I watch you alive but dead

In the Hospital

Eyes weary and red
Hair matted
Mouth quivering as if in a subzero winter's night
Slow eating
No eating
Bloody bandages
Bags of feces
Foleys filled with dark deep greasy pee
Tempers flaring
Feet stomping
Lips poked out
Love seems lost as I lay helpless
…. in the hospital

Nana

Your hair is as white as the snow
Your eyes are deep, cold and sad
Your hands are curled, twisted and painful
Your feet move slowly and deliberately as if the next step is your last.
Rush of anger flow like a broken barge
After days and months of locked silence
The constant jabs of pain make you scream
to go to your heavenly home.
Nana, Nana.. talk to me Nana
Lay down your burdens and let the water flow from those bewildered,
tired eyes cause I know you're at the end of your rope and
too frustrated and tired to care if today is
the day you meet your savior.

Nighttime in the Rural Bush

The quietness of the night calms my soul
and settles me into a private zone though
I'm aware of things around me
The screams and frivolous play of the crickets
Squirrels chirping as they playfully chase
each other up and down the trees
The energetic lizards that gracefully and swiftly slide across the porch
Cats that roam quietly around the house
claim their territory and their prey
Reindeer that gracefully enter as a family to
share a meal of young apples and tender pears
Fireflies that grace the night with their tiny lights dart
here and there in the night air
Stars that seem like they were thrown in place like chopsticks
The smell of smoke from rags burning to keep mosquitos away
Quiet chatter of neighbors sitting on their porches
because their houses are too hot inside
Sharing stories of great men and women and
their personal failures and successes
Its nighttime in the rural bush

Not a Choice

I'm married to a good little lady, while
trapped in a man's body
We have three little children depending on us
Secretly, I wear her clothes, shoes, earrings,
mascara and lipstick
I can't be manly and macho if I wanted to …
Angry at the world for making me keep my secret
Outside macho …inside tender
I'm struggling to be free and to be the woman that I am
But right now, it's my secret and not a
choice right now …not right now

Old Folk's Love

I'm happy that we made it through the years
Picking teeth with flossers
Chewing food with mouth open and smacking loudly
Snoring loudly through the night
digging boogers and dripping snot
belching long and deep
loud gas from derriere
yawning and coughing in my face
Shameless for days walking around without pants
Toenail shavings on the floor
Washing and crying about painful hemorrhoids
aching feet and legs
Old and still together
Yes, we made it through the years.
Old and still together.
Love is a camera full of memories.
Love is a bond.
Old and still together

Pocketbook Check

The inspecting officer in the emergency room entrance began
the inspection of my pocketbook. He saw...
Keys that open doors known and unknown
tissues(new and used)
coins and dollars
Sanitizers, wallet, pictures, old receipts
Leftover food from days and weeks
Bottle of water, candy, gum
forks, spoons, earrings, bills, letters, coupons for shopping, cellphone
notes, pens, pencils, finger nail file
lipstick, eyeglasses
He seemed afraid to put his hands deeper into my
pocketbook...looking as if his hands might be harmed
My pocketbook- a disaster area

Private Matters

Private Matters are embedded in the body and soul
like the deep roots of trees in the ground
Spreading in all directions and affecting near and far
They cause insecurities and doubts preventing the unleashing
of greatness Sleepless nights with bodies rolling like dice
rarely finding a good spot Head thumping like the beat
of a drum with each beat getting louder and louder
Painful pricks of needles radiating down my back, stomach and legs.
Private matters keep the mind in one zone, preventing
creativity, and energy ..zapping vitality and strength
Private matters are like a clock stuck in time
No more ticking.

Secrets

Secrets are like pebbles on the ocean floor
broken rocks under gigantic boulders
dirt in corners of floors
Spider webs underneath the legs of chairs
Bedbugs on mattresses
wax in the deepest part of the ear
continuous pain in a tooth
Dandruff in the hair follicles
Secrets are a ticking bomb, waiting to explode

Do It

It might take your classmate one hour to prepare for an exam
It might take you four hours .. Do not compare
Do it!
You might have to spellcheck each paragraph five times
If you do not want errors in your paper
Do it!
You might have to read the chapter six times
before you understand the information
Do it
Attend seminars, conferences and other learning
activities for personal and professional growth
Do it!
You might have to read the newspaper for
local, state and national news to
To be informed
Do it!
Be time conscious and show up on time
Do it
Empathize with people who are hurting and work
hard to develop a sweeter personality
Do it
Make service to others a part of your daily routine
Do it
Filter you words to prevent harshness
Do it
Wear the appropriate attire for the occasion. Find out before going
Do it
Believe in yourself and have faith in your abilities
Do it
Just Do It and shine

The Leaning Tree

I use to stand tall and strong with healthy, vibrant limbs
Very competent, wise, productive, and strong
My mind was sharp as a tack receiving, recycling and producing
Quality input into multi problems
Travelling through life's dark corridors and life changing trials and
Tribulations
I now am a leaning tree void of strength, beauty and stamina
Now nursed and cared for by a devoted and competent caregiver
Attending my needs all day and night
Her body grows weaker everyday as she lifts me, bathe me, dress me
Feed me and encouraged me during the day and night.
She rubs lotion on my aching body, exercise
my aching limbs, changed my
Soiled linen several times during the day and night. I see her
Tired eyes filled with tears and her back bent over and
legs moving slowly as she tends my every need.
I am the leaning tree and expected to meet
my savior soon, but as I look at
My tired, weak, strained caregiver, so frail and sickly, I
Realize that I, the leaning tree does not always fall first.

Silence

My tongue was motionless as if paralyzed
as I sat for hours, listening to words and more words,
expressions of the heart, deep wounds and moments of joy.
All of this came flowing quickly out like a
water hydrant with a large hole.
I took it all in and heard much pain,
then
Joy and hope filled the room
As forgiveness was requested and accepted
These experiences I will remember ..
I will remember all of it as I listened in total silence.

Simple Things

I feel incredible joy watching the squirrels hang on to the branches
of trees, ants working together ...traveling back and forth
collecting food and building safe homes under mounds of dirt.
Watching parents play with their children while laughing wildly
and sincerely with love visibly and enjoying their time together
Eating ice cream, drinking Kool aid
and eating a peanut butter and jelly sandwich
while the sunshine warms my body as I sit on the back porch
Simple things....good times

Stranger

They don't know my name, my family, or my history
but...
They call me hon, honey, sweetie, sweetie pie, dear, babe, darling
They don't know my name, they don't ask and they don't care
I'm a stranger

The Big "A"

The doctor said I could eat
with you, feed you, dress you, touch you, change your
bedsheets, breathe the same air... even kiss you.
But I don't know.... I don't know about this booger called AIDS.

The doctor said that I could encourage you,
reassure you
Give you unconditional positive regard
treat you with respect and dignity.
Allow you to express your feelings and desires but I don't
know.... I don't know about this booger called AIDS.

These Black Feet

These black feet count on others
to pray for me and on God to answer
Were steadfast against the fire hose and fierce dogs
had a mother who holds my head to her chest
had a grandmother whose eyes said pride and lips prayed
saw the common sense of my father
drank from the colored only fountain and worked
as maids, drivers, and farm hands
can still hear the wise advice of the village folks that raised me
These black feet stood in the unemployment lines for countless hours
have been loved even at my most unlovable times
walked through alleys and dark streets to
sell enough to feed the family
They have seen smiles and tears... courage and fears
followed the shadow of crooks
These black feet had a guardian angel all my life
before I could stand, before I could walk
and before I could speak
Have seen hard times
These black feet
walked with my mama as she cleaned the white
woman's house and cooked her food
washed loads of dirty clothes on the rub board
stomped and stomped seeds into the rich
dirt and produced bountiful food
chased lightning bugs to adorn my ears and fill my jar
These black feet are tired

Our Heavenly Father

When your days seem sad and dreary like a tree
split wide open and shattered by sharp
Strikes of lightening
When you can't seem to smile or laugh or move
after watching your home, your furniture,
Paintings, cars and memoirs vanish in flames
When your thoughts are dark and temptations great as
your lustful mind and eyes are fixed on another
When you want to hide behind locked doors as you
listen to the doctor say that you have AIDS
When you can't see the light at the end of the tunnel
as you see your arms and legs are now stubs
When your burdens are many and your friends are long gone
When your memory is gone and your days are
spent staring through the window
When you can't feel the sunshine on a hot sunny day
Just
Lean on him for he is stronger than the heaviest mountain
He helps the stressed, depressed, and hopeless
His heart runneth over with compassion and
he gives new mercies each day
You are his child and he loves you
He is our heavenly father

Trash Cans

If trash cans could talk
they would tell our life stories…
Rooms bought to share rushed love
Bills that are due and past due
Habits too gross to share
Foods we eat
Liquors we drink
Drugs we smoke, swallow, inject
Conditions we want to stay buried
Secrets, secrets and more secrets
If trash cans could talk

Unfaithful Angels

You control me so that I see and feel you
You pacify me so that I admire you
Dependent on you Ill forever be
Enhancing my wellbeing is not on your agenda
Unconditional positive regard- you never had
Non-possessive warmth you rarely show
Social justices- not a priority
Insensitive to my differences
In your presence, I feel less than pretty
As you pretend to know your stuff
No time to hear of discrimination, oppression or plain ol' hate
That keeps me low to the ground
Your eyes say that I was not included when abilities
and capacities for continued growth were distributed
No appreciation for my perspective and that I have no
personal qualities, abilities and resources to help myself
Faithful angels …Where are you?
Faithful angels…. Where are you?
Where are you my social worker?

Uniquely Gifted

Love for God
Unconditional love for others
Love for mate
Love extended family
Wise, compassionate, patient, humble, encouraging
Fearless, courageous, motivator, respectful of others
Lifelong learner, confidant
Unconditional positive regard
Logical and discerning
Excellent work ethic
Good listener
Leader
Team player
You are uniquely gifted in so many ways

Wasted

I can see Jack Daniel, Bacardi, Johnny Walker,
Boone's Farm, Morgan David and Red Dagger
I see weed and opiates
in your eyes
in your slurred speech and on your breath
in your loose tongue and twisted mouth
in your swayed stride
in your mind
Now ....you are unable to give and receive love
You hate yourself, me and others
Wasted

Aromatherapy

Rich and deep flavor tickle my nose. A smell no Cuban cigar
can compete with. Earthy with a subtle edge, I inhale deeply
to optimize the scent's full potential.
In a short time, I feel it in my head. Feeling full yet open of the mind,
I repeat the cycle, allowing the aroma to diffuse throughout the room.
I choose this therapy to deal with the daily
disappointments and frustrations
But this therapy session ends with a knock on the door as my 6 year
old son enters and asks me what that smell is?
Aromatherapy I say today.
But what do I say tomorrow?

Cheating Shoes

Shoes of all colors, sizes, real genuine leather, fake leather
Some cheap, others expensive and top of the line
Others from sticky fingers
Heels worn down, cracked and dull
others like they just came from the store
Some brand names, others no name
Some belong to wife cheaters
Others to partner cheaters
They come back and back and back again
and park their shoes beside my bed

Compassion Fatigue

I feel your pain, your heartache, your tears
as it clouds everything you do so you can't see clear
You are in the midst of your pain, your grief, your suffering
and then there's completely open and
empathetic but with no buffering
Your eyes say help and your voice feels urgent and wounded
As I listen to you with tenderness and an aching in my heart
I pour and pour light and hope into taking
no note regard to my own stores
or acknowledge they are few
You see I'm doing my best to be a rock for you
But I can't meet your needs, your demands,
your expectations because I myself am blue.
With you, it's always something new.
So I move forward without giving you a clue.....
that I am burned out, frustrated and depressed myself

Down Home Conversation

Food was real scarce so we went to bed
with half full bellies that talked loudly all night.
My sister had wind in her jaws as she complained
about her husband cheating with the woman down the road
and about his sister who pitched some fits and
painted her hair part yellow and part red.
I told him to red tag her and let her go....
because I didn't want him to get sick and bite the dust and because
whatever she's doing will come back and bite her in the butt.
She's a loose cannon. My cousin was always frazzled about every
little thing and bit the dust when he was only 30. He wanted his
lady to always be in his heart but she had other plans. He forgot
that all that glitters is not gold. She was definitely not gold.
He was mean hearted to so many and I told him
that he ought to be good to her cause he could catch
more flies with honey than with vinegar.
He said ok, but always was as nervous as a long
tail cat in a room full of rocking chairs.
How I love old folks down home conversation

Eyes

Black, blue, gray, green eyes
show happiness, sadness, grief, pain, hope and anticipation
others show pain and heavy burdens
Some are glassy, others red from the constant flow of tears
others are covered with sunglasses
and still others hide their pain filled eyes
with a happy mask
Eyes tell stories

Mary Jane

Unassuming, you look average.
Nothing special about you. Plain, not flashy.
Dull even.
I heard whispers about you.
So why not meet you.
Let me introduce myself.
But you were nice to me.
Treated me the way I always wanted to be treated.
I felt good around you. Lulled me asleep like a baby.
I dream bigger when I'm with you. I dance better.
You make me feel smarter. But sometimes when you're around,
I forget about everyone else. Time stops
for me, but goes on for everyone else.
People know when we've been together.
They say they can see it in my eyes,
the way I walk, The way I talk.
At least that's what the post office said before they fired me.
I don't blame you.
Its not your fault I lost my scholarship
It wasn't your plan to get me fired
Im sure you wanted me to fulfill my potential
You were just being you.
I simply fell in love with you, Mary Jane.

Dark Hours

In the dark, dark hours of night
Movies of past and present encounters
cascade one after another
Some sad, others happy
Some makes me want to scream and holler and run away

Others play flashbacks of love and tenderness and
then comes more silent time when I hear
the train from a distance, big delivery trucks trying to get to their
destinations to unload and cars rushing through the night to get home
to their love after loving someone else on the other side of town.

As time passes during the night with so much
pain and sadness, my eyes closed
I see the sun slowly hold its head up and then show
its full face all day only to stay until nighttime.

Fever

As my temperature rises to heights unknown
Sweat dripping out of every pore
Head pounding and ready to explode
Im not myself but out of control
As I cry out in anger with eyes bulging and fists balled
As I strike out at anyone and anything
and sharing secrets and names that are buried deep in my soul
I wildly pull off my clothes
unleashing me and exposing all of me
Like a newborn baby
Oblivious to eyes watching and ears listening
as this fever raged through my naked body

Hopeful Anticipation

In my mother's womb, I felt
Safe,
Warm
Loved
Beautiful
Hopeful
proud and happy

I dream of leaving my mother's womb
to enter the world and find
beauty
Warmth
Pride
Commitment
Love
Fairness
hope
faith and
Happiness

Instead, I found
hunger
persistent child poverty
wide gaps in wealth and income
Racial and sexual discrimination
oppression of women
Powerlessness
homelessness
hate crimes against gays and lesbians
Now I dream ....
Now I dream of returning to my mother's womb

The Real Me

In the still blackness of the night I itch from head to toe and scratch
until giant welts pop on my skin ... followed by a trail of red stuff.
This continues as the motion picture of my life dances before my eyes

Skeletons dance one by one as the pictures of my
life in all its color and trauma roll by
Pictures I locked away in a tiny capsule in my
mind...imprisoned for only me to know

I cringe and cry out for help and forgiveness as sweat
pours from my body like I have completed
a 10 mile run

I plead and plead for forgiveness as I am reminded
of the season of my life when I was lost and
sad and bewildered and had no one to direct me...to help me

I was afraid to allow any breathing human
beings to know how lost I was.
I live each day in agony of the day, the hours, the
minute when my secrets are no longer secrets
and my true soul, the real me is revealed.

What Happened?

What happened to....
Eating watermelons to the rind
Making homemade ice cream in a hand turning machine
Hanging clothes to dry on a clothes line
Cleaning the living room to receive visitors
Playing outside from morning to night
Coming in to the house before it gets night

What happened to......
Pouring molds of Jesus's face and fruits galore in vacation bible school
Learning Christmas and Easter speeches
wearing new shorts and tops for the 4th of July
New outfit for May day
to perform a dance on the maypole
Learning the scriptures from the Bible
Sitting on the mourning bench until the spirit touched our inner souls
Using rags in smoke fires to keep mosquitoes away

What happened to ...
Eating biscuits, chicken backs and fish heads for breakfast
Making sugar syrup
Baking squirrels and rabbits until soft and smothered in gravy
Eating cracklin bread and making peanut
butter and apple butter sandwiches
Making rice pudding out of left over rice

What happened to the good times?

Jaded Eyes

To me he was a knight in shining armor
Patient, loving, kind and trustworthy
Always at my beck and call
Always comforting and encouraging me
Showering me with praises and kudos
Saying that I deserve the best and all the rest
Treating others with respect
Helpful when needed
A generous heart
Intelligent and strong
A joyful spirit that never stops giving
But actually......
He was a liar and a cheater
A pimp and drug dealer during the night
A fake preacher man during the day
Married to two other women
He had hands that take and never give
But...
I couldn't see the real person because
I was looking through jaded eyes

I Am Me

I'm who I'm meant to be
I am my past, my present and who I want to be
I'm not anyone, I'm all of these
I am a work in progress, a destiny
I am who I choose to be
I am me

Sugar Daddy

He is twice my age
Walk slowly with humped shoulders
Dapper hat and pressed suits
Silver hair and sagging cheeks
Teeth that move up and down
He's my sugar daddy
Buys my groceries every week
Pays my house mortgage
Put some brand new clothes on my back
Maintenance for my car plus insurance
He's my sugar daddy
Energized by Viagra
He wants the back and neck rubs, leg rubs,then rubs all over
He has a hopeful glee in his eyes
As he downs the Viagra
And contemplates our sexual intertwine workout.
Life is a struggle. He is my life.
He's my sugar daddy…My sugar, sugar daddy

Frail

My tree roots are buried deep
in the dark earth
Sleeping peacefully for years while my trunk and branches stand
exposed to the harsh elements that test my tolerance for pain and
battering
As the cold wind pushes and the snow piles heavily
on my branches, I try to hold on and not break
Sometimes I stand still like an iron door and other times I snap
Under the pressure and break into unrecognizable pieces
I'm Frail

My Pain

My pain has taught me…
To pray
To be humble
To be generous
To understand others, their personal struggles and pain
To be loyal
To be compassionate
To be thankful
And not to be judgemental
Pain is upsetting, persistent and memorable
It hurts so much but I'm glad I have
Travelled the rocky road of pain after pain after pain
Now, I appreciate You my Lord
Now I appreciate the way you use my pain to bless me and others

Prayer for Ms. Lizzie

Lord,
Show mercy for my sweet mother-in-law
Protect this kind and giving woman
Who, has given, and continues to give…
To nurse, to encourage, to love so many
(sisters, brother-in-laws, nephews, nieces, mother-in-law, father-in-law,
mother, daughters and sons, grandchildren, great grandchildren)
Strengthen this great historian who has a wealth of family history
and events in her memory bank, always ready and willing to share.
Empower her with faith and courage that you will
watch over her while her eyes are closed
Give her confidence that you will guide the hand of the
surgeon. Let her feel our love and your warmth and let
her know you're beside her every minute, every second
through the procedure and during the healing phase.
Calm her quickly if doubt and fear begin to creep into her mind,
and remind her that you calmed the water during the storm,
protected Daniel in the lion's den and Jonah in the fish's stomach
Lord, I humbly ask these things for I know that you are
The **greatest physician**
The **greatest healer**
The **greatest protector**
Amen

Pretty Woman

I met a pretty woman with flawless skin
Plump, red lips
A coco-cola shape
Tits big and round
A boody.. wide and soft
She looked clean but she wasn't
Pretty woman, why didn't you tell me you had the "bug?"
Now I have the big "A"

Richly Endowed

You have given me beauty
Insight
Kindness
Humbleness
Generosity
Patience
Sensitivity
And a non-judgemental attitude
Thank you.. Now I feel richly endowed.

Revive Me

Shattered dreams and broken promises
When the sun comes up and goes down
Hard rocks falling like erupted volcanoes

Oh please dear Lord.. Revive me again
For those that are broken and torn and live in darkness
Make me a blessing to them
Revive me…Revive me Again

My Hair

Thick and long like fertilized grass
Thin, short, purple and black
Up or down, on the side or back
In knots or loose.
Braids or curls…afro or pressed
Sewed with perfect stitches or glued like masking tape
I'm trying to decide which one will please my boss
as he looks at me and my hair with a frown

We are Family

Mama's sick so you better come home
You need to stay for a month or two or more
Papa will be gone for a few years
Cause he stole some money from his job
And now lives in cellblock #40
The field needs tilling and the house repairing
Brother is out of work and needs another job
Just need a place to lay his head while looking for a job
Cousin Sam and wife just can't seem to make it
He needs a bed just for a few weeks
Just until he can get over the "blues"
Your sister Mattie's tummy is like a watermelon
And has no help
We'll put her up until the baby comes
Come on.. Come on cause we are family
We all get along and eat what we eat
Cornbread and buttermilk...biscuits and syrup
We'll all raise the children
Sweep the floors and slop the hogs
Cause we are all family

A Man's Testimony

Yes, I love men
And drop my pants for them
Yes, I snort the white devil's powder
And pump my veins with poisonous stuff
That makes me wild and angry and no good sense
Yes, I share needles with my buddies,...
Cause I can't afford new ones
Yes, I have sex with women of the night with ruby red lips like plums
And those that wear no panties
And no I don't have no money for the rubber
glove that covers my thang
When my rubber "break" I use it anyway cause I ain't got no money
Yes, I get the red thick blood flow into my body and swallow lots of
get well pills and yes, I'm paying the price for my escapades with
Lots of men, women and drugs

Call Me Cry Baby

Tuck your upper lip and deal with it.
Dry your eyes and hold your head up
Cause its all in your mind
Yes, mind over matter.... Its not that bad
No one else lives this pain
My true personality is not revealed as it is locked inside my body
and forbidden to interact with others. I am a prisoner in my skin.
Afraid to interact,
and be in the midst of the action.
The level of my pain is judged by others who think I don't have
much pain because I get up each day, bathe, get dressed, study
long hours, make good grades, and go to the movies each week.
When I talk about my pain, they call me cry baby.
That the pain in my head, is superficial and is not real.
Although my pain is real…they still call me cry baby.

My Panties

My panties lay wrinkled and quiet waiting to be grabbed by my hands
Some very aged with holes that marbles can slide through with ease
Others discolored from too many cycles in the washer
Others are new with the lingering odor of a Dollar Tree store
Colors bright, others faded
Some have become loose when the pounds came off
While others squeeze my boom boom
Panties could tell secrets if they could talk
But they are <u>MY</u> panties

A New Voice

My voice is silent now
I need a voice
To glorify God, the savior
To encourage the sad and distressed
The wayward, the lonely, the tired
And disgusted
I need a voice...
To remind the hopeless of his tender mercies
And forgiving nature
To call the sick and shut-in
To pray for his amazing grace
To express love for the Savior
To share examples of his miracles
I need a voice..be it weak or airy
Strong and clear to glorify God

Build Me Up

Build me up during my storms
Pray for me
Congratulate me
Love me
Encourage me
Teach me
Share my personal pain
Speak to me
Respond to my pain
Don't judge me
Don't close your eyes or turn your back on me
When I'm sick
When I'm down and out
When I'm dying
Help me.. Build me up

Mama's Secret

I'm just a little baby, I'm your little baby
Entering this big beautiful world
With high expectations and looking for hugs and kisses
Riding my bike
Playing with friends
Learning from the educated teachers
But since you had AIDS.. Now I have AIDS
Why didn't you tell me your secret?
Why didn't you Mama?

Rural is...

Spiritual, creative, communal, resourceful,
patient, hopeful, traditional, resilient,
Positive, cultural, peaceful, strong family ties,
Strong women, love of nature, pride, independent
Informal, loyal, energetic, faithful, and focused.
Value life, natural talent, teamwork, neighborly,
coping skills, well organized, isolation,
Violence, crime, low income.
Low educational attainment, little health insurance,
little access to specialty care services, little access to
emergency care, autonomy, patriarchal ideas,
Gender related roles, anonymity, victimization,
medically indigent and silent abuse

Rural...all these and more

No Exemption

Alaskan natives, Native Americans, Native Hawaiians, Blacks, Whites
AIDS stretches from one end of the globe to the other
The rich, poor, and in between
Men, women, and children
AIDS is my secret…
No one is exempt

Today

What did I do today for …
My mind?
My body?
My spirit?
My relationships?
My creativity?
My passion?
Others?

Today…. I'm working hard

Unmanly Man

I'm a man and suppose to be strong, the head of my house,
a leader, a decision maker, an example of strength
But…I'm weak, frail and timid
I'm threatened often, ridiculed daily, ignored, laughed
at, hit, kicked, slapped and called "little boy"
I have to stay home when I'm not working on my job
Can't spend time with my friends and family
Constantly accuses me of being unfaithful
Controls my time
Says I'm not important
When I'm with her I shake like a leaf on a strong windy day
Like a naked child standing in the bitter cold winter day
I'm a man so I'm embarrassed to report the abuse
So I suck it all in and fill my body with liquor and drugs
As I keep my secret life a secret

Imperfections

When you look at me... you can see me
I can't stand up straight and tall because I m structurally
weak from harsh, roaring winds and heavy snow
From heavy swings and hammocks
From the relentless saws of tree cutters and
smearing of black tar to retard my growth
When you look at me, you can see ...
Indentions made by the teeth of rodents
and worms and other parasites
Green decayed fungus and mold like blotches that
sucked the life out of my woody tissues
Deep cavities and rotten branches
Seams and wide cracks made from storms have
blemished, freckled and twisted my trunks
You can see all of me when the leaves no longer grow.
All of my perfect imperfections.
I'm naked now.
I am like the tree- You can see me. Teeth missing, head down
and drooping shoulders, bones aching, anguish, boredom, a
strange silence with my perfect imperfections, waiting for care.

Strength

Like the strong oak that does not bend nor
bow to the ferocious wind, the cold
Rushing water and the weight of accumulated
ice and snow…You do not bow
To mediocrity and convoluted situations.
You stand
Like the beautiful, strong, diverse branches of the oak,
Your outstretched arms spread out like wings of an eagle in
All directions to help…the torn and the tattered….
The abused and misused…..the down and out…. The peon,
The disenfranchised and marginalized men,
women, and children…..near and far
You reach
Like the embedded roots of the oak provides
Protection from the weather and predators…
You provide protection for people through your
love, compassion, and kind deeds.
You support
Like the oak that lives and has a grand presence in every season
You choose to enjoy each season and be content
You choose to enjoy the moment, to see the good in
people and things, and to embrace the beauty.
You thrive
Like an oak tree.. you stand, you reach, you support, you thrive
Like a beautiful, strong, majestic oak tree

Discrepancies

Cheating spouse.. but want a stable marriage
Yelling spouse. .but want a strong marriage
Neglecting my children .. but I love them
Want to keep my job but I'm absent a lot of days
Want a degree but I don't study
Want a neat house but clothes and trash are everywhere
Speed when driving but don't want a ticket
Drinking and smoking pot but don't want to be arrested
Want some help from the therapist but I don't show up
Visibly drunk but I don't want a DUI on my record
Want to be an engineer but I don't like math
Criticizing but don't want to be criticized
Behavior offends and alienates others but don't
want to be offended and alienated
Want to be a social worker but don't like people
Want love but can't love
Want, want, want but can't get it until I put in the time
Life is a journey… sometimes smooth…sometimes rocky..
So many DISCREPANCIES

Love and Gratitude to My Soul Mate

Happy Birthday to one of my favorite people
Thanks for being here… for being you
I am so glad you are on this earth
I hope you feel loved and appreciated today because you are.

Thanks for being wonderful
Thanks for being you.
With love that will never stop growing
Oceans of love to my soul mate.
Thanks Budie!

Grandma's Words

You can't hold water
(You can't keep a secret)

It's like taking a knife to a gun fight
(Useless, you don't have a chance)

Like water rolling off a duck's back
(Does no good to give advice because the person won't listen)

Red tag her and let her go
(Can't do anything with her)

My mind fell on you
(You are on my mind)

What you say?
(Really?)

You won't miss your water til your well run dry
(You will not miss a good thing until it's gone)

He's like a wolf in sheep's clothing
(Deceptive, pretending to be something that he's not)

He's as nervous as a long tail cat in a room full of rocking chairs
(Full of anxiety, very anxious, very nervous)

She'll steal sugar out of gingerbread
(real good at stealing)

Running Through the Trees

I see magnolia trees, cedars, pecan trees,
weeping willows, and dogwood trees
Standing tall and strong
But Limbs that are too weak to hold on to the trees
lay lifeless, fragile and discolored on the ground
Reminds me of sick children too weak to hold on to their mother
I see bricks used as a safe home for snakes
I see squirrels nibbling on morsels of food buried in the dirt
I see deep holes in the ground used as a home for gopher rats
Cats standing quietly eyeing the gopher hole
waiting patiently for the prey
I see mama deer and her babies nibbling leisurely on the pears
that fell on the ground and those still dangling on the trees
Beer cans and liquor bottles hiding in torn bags
Dirty paper and wet trash in a trail
Water flowing swiftly in a ditch
I saw all of these and more while I was running through the trees

Footprints of Good Woman

Love God and unfailing belief in God
A giver of self and deeds
Trustworthy and kind spirit
A prayer warrior
Put love into action
An encourager
Have hands that help
Intuitive, intelligent, strong
A joyful spirit that touches others
A generous heart and soul
Live her faith
Shares her time and talent with others
Sacrifice for others
Comforting others when needed
Dependable
Challenge, praise, guide, inspire others
Genuine concern
Warmth and sincere
Unconditional Love
Respectful to others
Patience
Express appreciation

My Butterfly

I poured my life and love into you
Filling you up like a pitcher of sweet punch
Nourishing like fertilizer mixed in rich soil growing a beautiful flower
Making sure you have the skills to survive
Making sure you have the skills to fly and succeed
Making sure you have the courage to shine
You were cocooned with strength, reliability and trust
Now you show your vibrant colors…prancing
through life brightly and proudly
Caring more, giving more, loving more
Weasel
My beautiful strong butterfly

My Sunshine

The strings of her heart are tied to many people
A member of a family of believers
Always Praying for others
Confidence in God when the world seems out of control
Words of assurance of God's love given to the down and out
A character of honor
Perseverance when problems arise
Richly blessed with Godly virtues of patience, kindness and love
Armed with God's word and compassion
Clean motives in her heart
Gifts of honesty, kindness and empathy from God
Unconditional love
A heart devoted to God, family and friends
The Lord, a source of her strength
Modeling love of God to others
Cheerful and radiant spirit
Calmness during storms of life
God's angel on earth, My Gussie

The Woods

My mind scattered like broken marbles
From Daily trials and tribulations
I wipe the rolling tears from my cheeks as I slowly take step
after step and find myself in a dark cocoon of quietness.
I can't see the sunshine since the once blue sky is now
interlocking green and brown tree heads only allowing
the darkness within and saying no to the sunshine
So peaceful in my space
I hear the wind blowing, squirrels cracking the hard hickory nuts
Birds singing and chirping and feeling safe under the blanket of trees
Snakes nesting in the damp dirt
Gopher rats hiding quietly under the brown leaves that
served as a safe blanket for privacy and prey
To prevent breaking my legs, I step gingerly over
Ditches, ravines, slick rocks and wide roots hidden by deep
blankets of leaves, limbs, briars, spider webs and debris
Disguising the magnitude of their depth
Slick rocks covered with green moss and mold
Man against nature I see vividly
I feast on big, juicy plums, black berries and nuts while I
continue to enjoy the peace and tranquility in the woods
Before returning to the hectic pace outside my cocoon.

About the Author

God sometimes blesses his people as children to what their mission in life will be. Shelley Wyckoff was one of those people. It was imprinted in her mind that she would be a Social Worker before she fully knew what the words meant. From 11 years old and on, God began preparing her to implement her mission, serve Him through service to humanity utilizing the profession of social work as the conduit. Her life has been characterized by giving of self and personal caring. A continuous gardener, she has been sewing seeds of hope, confidence, faith, and self assurance from early on. This book contains a small look at the essence of the spirit of a social worker for life in life. This collection of poetic life expressions is realistic, raw, gripping, moving and thought provoking. Shelley Wyckoff was born and raised in Bessemer, Alabama. She is one of eight children born to James and Anna Lee Rice. While a young child, she was a babysitter for relatives. In high school and college Shelley was an academic achiever and worked during the summers at factories in New York and Ohio. Her undergraduate college education at Tuskegee Institute was funded through work-study programs. She continued her education by receiving a master's degree in social work from Atlanta University and a Doctorate of Education from Vanderbilt University. Dr. Shelley Wyckoff is professor emeritus of the Alabama Agricultural and Mechanical University Department of Social Work. Before retiring in June 2011, she served in various administrative positions as Director of Field Instruction, Director of the Undergraduate Social Work Program and Chair of the Department of Social Work. She has served as a site visitor for the Council on Social Work Education and a Commissioner of Accreditation. She was inducted in the 2011 Alabama Social Work Hall of Fame.

Printed in the United States
By Bookmasters